MEMORIES OF OLDHAM

D1244252

TRUE NORTH BOOKS

DEAN CLOUGH
HALIFAX
WEST YORKSHIRE
HX3 5AX
TEL 01422 344344

THE PUBLISHERS WOULD LIKE TO THANK THE
FOLLOWING COMPANIES FOR SUPPORTING THE
PRODUCTION OF THIS BOOK

BRITISH AEROSPACE

BRITISH VITA PLC

CHADWICK WEB PROCESSING PLC

THE OLDHAM COLLEGE

S. FRANKENHUIS & SON LIMITED

GEORGE HILL (OLDHAM) LIMITED

J.W. HUMPHREYS & SONS LIMITED

KNOLL SPINNING COMPANY LIMITED

J.W. LEES & COMPANY (BREWERS) LIMITED

LEES-NEWSOME

OLDHAM MARKET

OLDHAM MOTOR COMPANY LIMITED

PLATT & HILL LIMITED

ROXY CINEMA

SHILOH PLC

SIEMENS MEASUREMENTS LIMITED

THE SPINDLES SHOPPING CENTRE

SOUTH EAST LANCASHIRE HOUSING ASSOCIATION LIMITED

TOWN SQUARE SHOPPING CENTRE

FRANK WARREN LIMITED

EMANUEL WHITTAKER LIMITED

WRIGLEY CLAYDON

First published in Great Britain by True North Books
Dean Clough
Halifax HX3 5AX
1998

© TRUE NORTH HOLDINGS
ISBN 1 900 463 76 8

Introduction

Welcome to Memories of Oldham, a nostalgic look back on the people, places and events which shaped the town over half a century. Our aims have been similar to those which guided the production of our first Oldham book, Bygone Oldham; entertainment takes priority over serious study, though the pages are liberally sprinkled with interesting facts, anecdotes and comment where appropriate.

Many local companies have allowed us to recount the history of their organisation on these pages, and fascinating reading it makes too. Oldham has an impressive record where industry is concerned, not just in the area of textiles, for which it is obviously best known, but

Oldham's bustling Tommyfield Market in the 1960s

in a whole host of other business pursuits, many of which are described here. The Victorian men of vision gave us some beautiful buildings and created the wealth which enabled Oldham to grow and prosper. We have not, however, forgotten the countless thousands of ordinary men and women with their own brand of gritty determination, who worked so hard in the mills and factories to make all this prosperity possible.

In common with most towns and cities, particularly in the north of England, Oldham has undergone many changes during this time. The impact of these changes on the lives of ordinary people seems easier to comprehend with the benefit of a decade or two's hindsight. The various developments were not always welcomed by the people they were supposed to help, but change was inevitable as a consequence of changing circumstances and a changing world. The growing level of car ownership, increasing prosperity and the demands of national retail chains were all catalysts which meant that wholesale changes to the architecture of Oldham were inevitable. Changes in the popularity of various forms of entertainment, particularly with the demise of cinema-going in the late 1950s and 1960s would add to the impetus for change, as did the major reorganisation of the public transport system.

The clearance of substantial areas of poor quality housing was a contentious issue in Oldham, as it was in most other thriving industrial areas. Everyone wanted

to get rid of the damp, insanitary housing and communal outside toilets, but there was to be less enthusiasm for the high rise developments and sometimes impersonal estates which replaced them. Much of the development work which took place in the 1940s and 1950s was extensively photographed, and we have been fortunate to gain permission to reproduce the best ones in this book.

Change is taking place constantly in our town, and, inevitably, our sense of perspective depends largely on our age and the experiences we have enjoyed... and endured. As we get older it is often easier to 'step back' and view the events which have shaped our lives in a clearer light. Of course, we are always pleased when readers write to us with their own memories of the places we feature so that we can add to the detail in future publications.

It is our hope that the photographs and text contained in the following pages will rekindle a memory or two for you in an entertaining manner, bringing back to life the sights, sounds and atmosphere of times not so long ago. Whatever your age and interest in the town, we hope you enjoy reading this nostalgic backward glance at the Oldham we used to know and love. Happy Memories!

Phil Holland
True North Books

COVER DESIGN/PHOTOGRAPHS COMPILED BY MARK SMITH
CAPTIONS COMPILED BY PHIL HOLLAND AND PAULINE BELL
TEXT PAGES DESIGNED BY MANDY WALKER AND NICKY BRIGHTON
LOCAL BUSINESS CONTENT ORGANISED BY ANDREW HALES

Contents

Right: A tremendous effort went into this illuminated display at the Town Hall to celebrate the coronation of His Majesty George VI and Queen Elizabeth (now the Queen Mother) in 1937. The picture was taken on the night of a coronation ball at the Town Hall, and there was much dancing at other venues throughout Oldham during the week.

Events & occasions

Above: There are some stern looks in this picture which was taken by the spinning machines at Orb Mill. Its purpose was clearly to record some national celebration or other, judging by the bunting and paper flags of various nationalities strewn across the room, and it probably dates from the 1920s. There is quite a wide range of ages in the picture; the little lass standing virtually in the centre of the scene appears to be no more than 12 years old, while the white-haired lady second from the right would have been heading for retirement. We can't help wondering what happened to the group in the turbulent years that followed their photograph - and we would be delighted to hear from anyone who can enlighten us. Orb Mill was built on Holgate Street by the Orb Mill Company Ltd., in 1907. It was enlarged in 1941 but ceased production 20 years later in 1961. The building was later acquired by I.C.I and put to use as a wallpaper manufacturing mill.

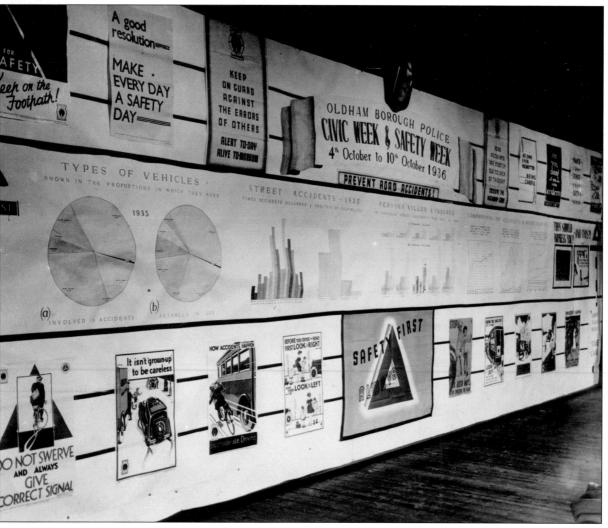

Left: A delightful scene which was recorded almost three quarters of a century ago in 1932. The proud mothers and lovely children are members of the Oldham Baby Clinic at Werneth Park. It is a sobering thought to consider that even the smallest of the children in the photograph will be around retirement age today. In August 1932 186 Wakes Week clubs distributed £168,653 to members on the Wakes Saturday - and there were over 400 weddings during the week! Later in the year a vote was organised on the question of opening Picture Houses on Sundays. The result was 3227 votes in favour and 12,092 votes against.

Below left: Oldham Borough Police Civic Week and Safety week had the catchy heading "Prevent Road Accidents" but despite this the event proved a huge success. The advertising experts had obviously been working overtime to come up with slogans such as "Don't swerve and always give the correct signal"

and "It isn't grown-up to be careless." The picture dates from 1936.

Below: Safety Week in 1936 was primarily concerned with safety on the roads. The event was intended to raise public awareness of the perils associated with motorised transport - from a pedestrian's point of view as well as that of the increasing band of motorists. Many people today are surprised to learn that the death toll on Britain's roads in modern times is almost half that of the 1930s, despite the fact that there are now many more vehicles on the roads. The reasons for this are many, and include the more efficient and safer design of modern motor vehicles, better road layout, legislation (such as drink-driving laws), better driving tuition and many other modern safety improvements. We shouldn't be complacent, but we should remember that not everything in the past was better than it is today.

Below: It was estimated that 40,000 people turned out to welcome Sir Winston Churchill when he visited Oldham in June 1945. The great wartime leader is seen here with microphone in hand at the West Street site of the town, standing on the platform with the two prospective M.Ps he had come to support. Prior to this public address, Churchill had driven through the town, standing in an open-topped car, to the delight of thousands of well-wishers who lined the streets. Outside the Town Hall he commented "this is where I fought my first campaign." Pointing to the building he said "this is the place where I was told I was out... and later that I was in." These comments referred to the first time that Churchill had fought for a seat in Parliament in the 1899 election, when he lost, and his success in the so-called 'Victory' election of 1900. He went on: "When I came back from the South African War they gave me a wonderful reception and took me through the streets in a horse-drawn carriage. The reception you have given me today exceeds the one you gave me in my youth." This might have been wishful thinking on the part of Churchill because newspaper reports from the time described how booing was heard at the West Street site when the great leader was speaking. Churchill was made a Freeman of the Borough in 1941 but never returned to the town to collect the honour.

"OLDHAM CIVIL DEFENCE CORPS WAS THE FIRST TO HAVE ITS OWN ORCHESTRA"

Above: Many of us remember attending childhood parties like this one. This picture depicts a childrens' party dating from 1960. It had been organised by the Oldham Civil Defence Corps for the offspring of the membership. This was part of their overall campaign to make membership attractive to adult recruits - and once recruited the wide range of social activities was one of the mechanisms for retaining staff. In the area of social activity the Oldham C.D.C excelled. It was the first *Corps* in the country to have an orchestra and the first to have its own social club. In terms of more direct recruitment activity they were the first organisation of their type to conduct door to door canvassing for new members. This group of well-behaved youngsters look very well turned out for their party. But try making *your* little lad wear a tank top, and a tweed jacket these days..... let alone a tie!

Below: A damp Sunday afternoon in 1945 saw the Victory Parade pass the Town Hall with Alderman Haywood the Mayor of Oldham taking the salute. Grey skies and heavy showers could not dampen the tremendous public display of happiness as thoughts of peace and a return to normal civilian life replaced the anxiety and hardship of wartime. The parade was headed by a police patrol car and two motorcycle outriders, closely followed by the Moston Colliery Band. Representatives from over 20 organisations, military and civilian, took part in the march and the A.T.C band played in front of the Town Hall for most of the procession.

Right: The factory workers at AVRO played an essential part in the production of aircraft during the Second World War and, as a consequence, were the subject of several highly-publicised visits form various celebrities and V.I.Ps during the six year conflict. One of the most popular visitors to the AVRO plant during this time was the wife of the President of The United States, Mrs. Eleanor Roosevelt. America's First Lady insisted on meeting as many workers as time would allow, and her kind, interested and relaxed style won many compliments from the factory staff. A lunch was held in Mrs. Roosevelt's honour, after which she insisted on meeting the canteen manager to ask for the recipe for the *excellent* apple pie she had just enjoyed. There was a particular sense of sadness among the workforce of AVRO when, shortly before the end of the war news came that President Roosevelt had died.

Below right: The end of the war was the signal for country-wide celebrations. The occasion was marked in the town with street parties, bunting, flags, bonfires, dancing and the illumination of mills and public buildings. Specially illuminated 'V' signs were erected by the score around the town, including one at Hartshead Pike which flashed its Victory message across the district every few seconds. Fireworks, which had been stored by individuals since before the war, were brought out and let off enthusiastically. In Alexandra Park a bonfire was lit soon after midnight on V.E Day. The Victory Parade seen in this picture took fully twenty minutes to pass the Town Hall where the salute was being taken by the Mayor of Oldham, Alderman Haywood. Most people agreed that it was worth braving the raindrops to be present at such an historic event.

"REPORTS WARNED OLDHAMERS NOT TO FLY THEIR UNION FLAGS UPSIDE DOWN"

'Victory Week' the series of celebrations held to mark the end of the Second World War, was generally bright and sunny, apart from the climax of the week, the parade through Oldham town centre on the Sunday afternoon. Reports in the Oldham Evening Chronicle warned Oldhamers not to fly the Union Flag upside down during the celebrations. Keen-eyed observers had spotted flags being flown the wrong way up at various points through the town and certain people were incensed by it. The paper stated: " The Union Flag should always be flown with the broad white stripe nearest the flagstaff. The only time it should be flown upside down is in dire emergency, in times of shipwreck or mutiny. So fly your flag the right way up - to do otherwise is an insult!"

Inset: The street lighting and clock department of Oldham Borough Council created this display for the 1949 Local Government Exhibition. The exhibition was held at the Drill Hall on Rifle Street between 8th October and 15th October. It was opened by the Rt. Hon. George Tomlinson M.P the Minister for Education at the time who talked about the need to overcome the great apathy shown by local people during council elections. Advertisements in the local press described the many attractions which could be found at the event. These included 'historical exhibits' and working models, as well as a 100 horsepower diesel motorbus engine, an original 1725 Oldham Fire Appliance and a police patrol car with a working two way radio crammed into the boot.

Main picture: Many organisations took part, not just Council departments. In this picture several well-known organisations, including British Railways and The Co-operative Wholesale Society can be seen supporting the exhibition which was the focal point of the centenary celebrations. Exhibits included 'mechanical accounting machines', gas and electricity appliances, film shows and refreshments. There was controversy over the issue of admission charges which had initially been set at one shilling (5p) for adults and sixpence for children. After a week the charges were dropped altogether, a statement from the Council suggesting that, on reflection, it had been decided that it was considered more important to get as many people through the 'turnstiles' as possible than to use the event to raise money.

This picture has been selected because it is typical of the impromptu street decorations and parties in Oldham and district which accompanied the coronation of Her Majesty Queen Elizabeth II in June 1953. The photograph records a scene at Birch Avenue, Chadderton and shows an impressive portrait picture of the Queen being used as the centrepiece of this street's decorations. The coronation is remembered for many celebrations and a sense of national rejoicing which had rarely been seen before or since. One milestone associated with the event involved television, for the coronation was instrumental in creating a major upsurge in demand for the new technological miracle that most of us take for granted now. The first television pictures had been received in Oldham on November 15th 1949. Remarkably they had been transmitted from Sutton Coldfield in the Midlands during a short test. Engineers were impressed with quality when they viewed them at Butterfield's (Yorkshire Street), The Music Box (Mumps), and C.H Wood of Curzon Street. One Mr Shatwell of Raper Street, Waterhead was experimenting with his homemade television receiver when he picked up the transmission. The age of television had arrived, but it would not be until the 1960s when more than half the houses in the Borough owned a set.

Above: The visit to Oldham by Her Majesty Queen Elizabeth II and HRH the Duke of Edinburgh in 1954 was cause for much celebration throughout the town. The royal couple arrived in Oldham as part of an extensive tour of Lancashire. At this time, just a year or so after the coronation, the royal family was enjoying tremendous popularity. Remember too, that in the days before there was widespread access to television sets, the opportunity to get a real-life view of the monarch would have been grasped with enthusiasm. Her Majesty looks youthful and radiant in this photograph, and by this time she had been married to the Duke of Edinburgh for seven years. It was a damp day for the visit, though this did not diminish the warmth of the welcome given to the royal party by the people of Oldham. Notice how, unusually, we can see the Queen carrying her own umbrella in this photograph.

> ## "THE QUEEN VISITED OLDHAM IN 1954 AS PART OF AN EXTENSIVE TOUR OF LANCASHIRE"

Below: Months of preparation went into the arrangements for the visit to Oldham of Her Majesty Queen Elizabeth II in October 1954. The visit also took in Shaw and the royal party found time to visit Lilac Mill for a tour that everyone who worked there would always remember. The royal motorcade is about to arrive outside the Town Hall in this picture, the elegant Rolls Royce closely followed by a robust Daimler saloon. The weather was unkind during Her Majesty's short stay but the thousands of cheering subjects didn't seem to mind too much. A special wooden stand had been constructed outside the Town Hall with seating for Oldham's Councillors and important V.I.Ps. Notice the determined-looking military Guard of Honour in the photograph. They look like a force to be reckoned with, having small arms at the ready - just in case.

At leisure

Below: This picture is thought to date from the 1940s and features the Oldham Police Football Club. The discipline was rugby football of course, though each of the players in the photograph generally has a smaller build than we would normally expect to see in modern competitors.

"THE BOXING DAY, 1935 MATCH BETWEEN OLDHAM ATHLETIC AND TRANMERE ROVERS RESULTED IN DEFEAT FOR THE HOME SIDE"

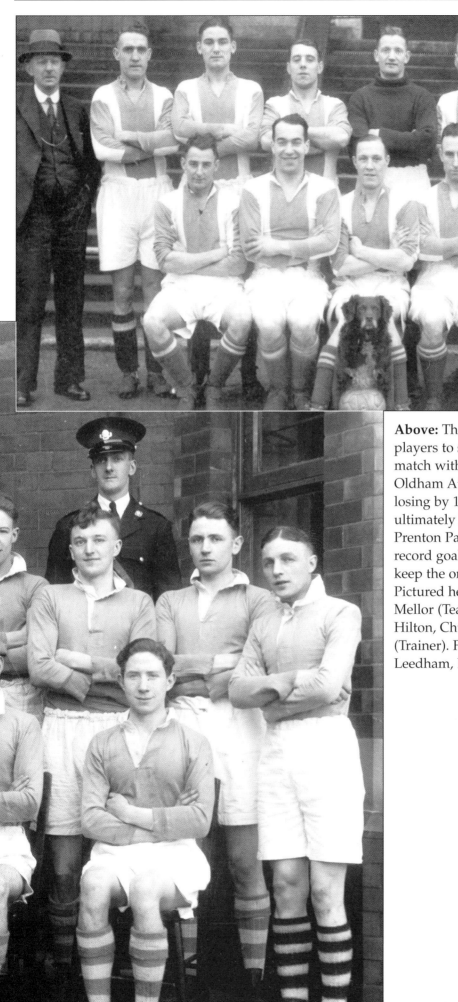

Above: There really wasn't much for these players to smile about after their Boxing Day match with Tranmere Rovers back in 1935. Oldham Athletic sustained a record defeat, losing by 13 goals to 4 in the high-scoring but ultimately highly embarrassing game at Prenton Park. Even the presence of Athletic's record goal scorer Tommy Davies could not keep the on-form Tranmere team at bay. Pictured here are (back row, left to right) Mellor (Team Manager), Gray, Brunskill, Hilton, Church, Seymour, Robson, Tufnell (Trainer). Front row: Agar, Davies, Walsh, Leedham, Buckley.

Below: The 'jewel in the crown ' of Oldham's civic resources is the beautifully laid-out Alexandra Park. The sight of this broad promenade will bring back happy memories for many readers. It dates from 1941 and features these five 'young ladies' enjoying the sunshine and the tranquillity of the clean open spaces on this warm summer's day. Alexandra Park first opened on August 28th 1865 and covered an area of around 70 acres. The total cost to the ratepayers of Oldham was around £31,000 and represented one of the best investments in the health and recreational pleasures of Oldhamers that the town has ever seen. It was a welcome oasis away from the crowded, dirty central area of town that many ordinary folk had to endure.

Right: A hive of activity at Grotton Lido can be seen in this picture which was taken around sixty years ago. Grotton Lido was a huge draw to people young and old (but mainly young) whenever the temperature rose high enough to take your overcoat off.

The combination of hot sunshine and cool water was irresistible. There won't be too many Oldhamers left who are able to remember the pleasures of the Lido in the years running up to the outbreak of the Second World War, but those who do tell tales of the shrieks, the splashes, the picnics and the long walks home after a days' fun at this much-loved facility. Lovely!

Below right: George Hardwick was Oldham Athletic's dashing young player-manager in the early 1950s. In this photograph he has more than a passing resemblance to Clark Gable and Errol Flynn as he speaks to a meeting of the Oldham Athletic Supporters' Club at Hill Stores in 1952. Hardwick's great claim to fame was that he captained every side that he played in - including the England national side which he led at the peak of his playing career. He was also the youngest ever player-manager when he was engaged by the Oldham Club in November 1950.

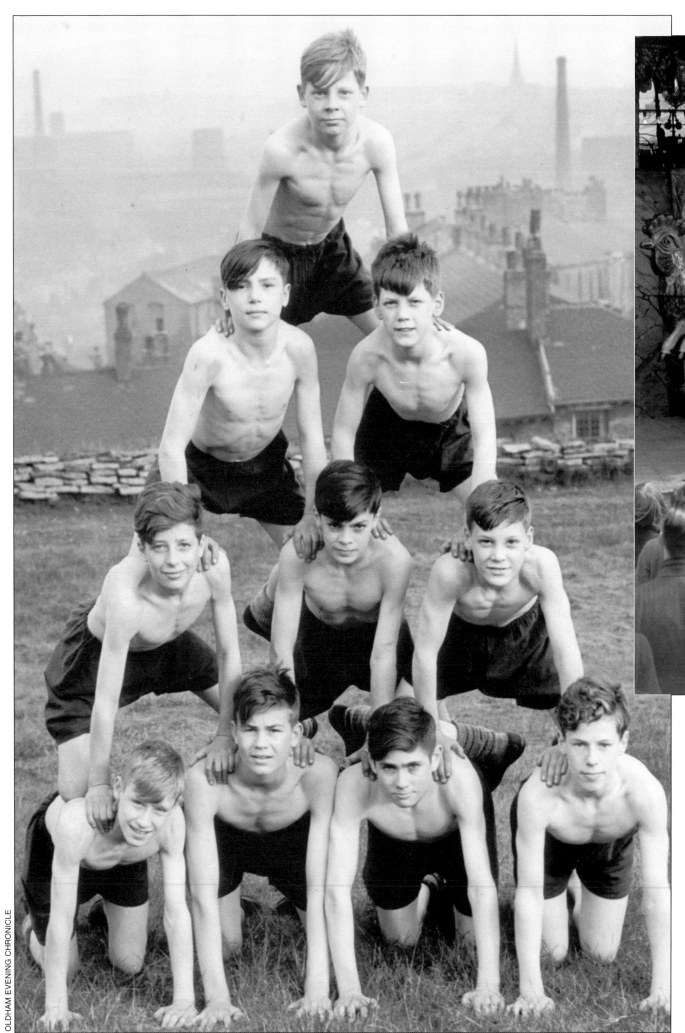

OLDHAM EVENING CHRONICLE

Left: You had to make your own entertainment in *those* days. This scene dates from the 1950s and features ten lean young lads in 'pyramid' formation on the outskirts of the town centre. We know precious little about who the lads are (though, as usual, we would be delighted to hear from anyone who might enlighten us) but they look as if they might be members of a boys' club or other youth organisation. These were the days when climbing trees, playing football in the street, a swim in the canal or mill pond were the favoured kinds of entertainment. It was a time when 'being sent to your room' was a form of punishment, unlike today where most parents find it hard to get their kids *out* of their rooms, thanks to the wonders of central heating, portable televisions and computer games.

Above: There was lots to do at Wakes Week in Oldham, even if you could not afford to get away on holiday. The main attraction in town was, of course, the Oldham Fair. Always well attended, and more often than not good humoured, it provided a welcome annual diversion from the rigours of daily life for generations of local folk. This press photograph features the Mayor of Oldham and some of his officials in the early 1950s, taking advantage of ride on one of the mot popular attractions. At around the time this picture was taken *Wakes Week* itself was in the news. After a long campaign by the United Textile Factory Workers Association it was agreed to add an extra week to the wakes' entitlement. This applied to 300,000 industrial cotton workers, many of whom lived or worked in Oldham. The first two-week wakes holiday took place from June 21 1952.

Above: A park wouldn't *be* a park without a boating lake! Alexandra Park's boating lake was a later addition to the rest of the facility, opening as it did in 1903 at a cost of nearly £14,000. Most people would judge this to have been a wise investment. And many readers will have fond memories of their first uncertain journeys across the broad expanse of water in days gone by. The first time dad let us take the oars ourselves, or a romantic trip with a young man or lady on board would create a mental record that would stay with us for ever. This delightful photograph recreates the tranquil atmosphere of the gently lapping waters, but the chimneys and terraced houses were never too far away and can be seen here beyond the stout, broad-leaved trees on the perimeter of the park.

Right: The 1949 Borough Centenary celebrations included many social events designed to appeal to both young and old. This picture features the 'Centenary Stage Show' which was staged for this enthusiastic audience of young children. Oldham was incorporated as a Borough in 1849 and in 1888 it was one of the County Boroughs named in the Local Government Act of the same year. In the century up until this picture was taken the population of Oldham had quadrupled.

This tremendous picture shows staff from the Oldham Co-operative Society in June 1960. The photograph was taken to record a staff outing to the Cadbury Brothers chocolate confectionery works at Bourneville in the Midlands. Staff social activities such as this one seemed to be far more commonplace in the 1950s and 60s; this was an era, unlike the present time, when most people expected to join a firm at an early age and remain there until retirement. They were times when tea-boys could work their way up through a company to the most senior positions - though female staff found it much harder to progress in the male- dominated world of work.

Below: This picture dates from 1951 and features the Market Place area of Oldham as it was about to undergo a major transition. Three weeks work for a 16 strong Council workforce was involved with the aim of cutting out some of the most severe bends on the route through this part of town. Four of the original traffic islands were done away with, three new ones were created, the largest being 170ft long and 70ft wide. Notice the popular public house the Prince William of Gloucester (known locally as the 'Top Drum') and the sign on the left of the picture advertising the 'new' Belle Vue in Manchester.

Around the town centre

Above: An almost artistic night-time view of High Street which is thought to date from 1946. Tram lines are still present along this, one of Oldham's busiest streets; they were removed in August 1946 with the demise of the trams. That occasion was marked by the running of an illuminated tramcar, driven by the Mayor, Alderman S.T. Marron from Waterhead to Hollinwood to the delight of cheering crowds lining the route. At the peak of the tram era, in 1927, there were 122 tramcars on the routes throughout Oldham.

Above: A late 1930s view of Market Place featuring the distinctive white stonework of the Burton's Building. Most towns of any note had a Burton's and generations of local folk would find this a ready source of wedding suits, clothes for everyone's *Sunday best*, and smart attire for all occasions. Britain's best-known tailors first began trading in Oldham in 1914. The area of Oldham depicted in this photograph was once the hub of retail activity in the town. Shops of many different types, including clog makers, chemists, grocers, butchers - along with many public houses, were crammed into the vibrant commercial area. Unlike today it was normal for busy shopping areas like this to be densely populated too, with the large families of the shop owners living either above, or beneath the shops themselves. This picture clearly shows the tramlines and overhead power cables which still ran along the busy thoroughfare. Less than ten years after this picture was taken the tramway era would come to an end.

Below: Many decades of soot and other airborne pollution had caused black staining on the walls of Union Street's fine old buildings. This picture dates from the dawn of the 1960s, a time when serious moves towards cleaner, healthier air were getting under way throughout Britain with the Clean Air Act which would result in 'smokeless zones' being introduced compelling businesses and householders to use only 'smokeless' fuels or make the conversion to gas or electric power. The dignified building on the right is the Lyceum which opened in 1856. It was extended in 1881 and the full effect of the stylish facade is visible today thanks to the extensive sandblasting carried out some years ago. The almost Gothic styling of the Prudential Assurance building can be seen further along the street and the white dome of the Grosvenor Cinema can be seen in the distance. That building has since been pulled down, replaced by the Job Centre. Every town had its 'Monkey Run' and Oldham was no exception. Union Street had the distinction of being the place where hopeful young people would 'strut their stuff' in the hope of meeting their ideal partner.

Above: Feelings of pure nostalgia are captured in this delightful scene from the 1950s. A comfortable bench surrounded by raised flower beds and tubs, in the middle of the busy shopping area provides an oasis of calm for three elderly gents, no doubt discussing some of the changes that they had seen over the years. Everything looks neat and tidy in this view, not a hint of graffiti in sight (in fact, the term 'graffiti' was not even in common use at this time) unlike most pieces of 'street furniture' we pass on modern streets. This part of High Street was the location of William Deacon's Bank, seen here on the right. The picture is given added character by the curvaceous motorcars and commercial vehicles, rather commonplace at the time, but now highly collectable as people begin to value the simple, but endearing designs of the past.

"THE IMPORTANCE OF MARKET PLACE AS A SHOPPING AREA HAS GROWN WITH THE BUILDING OF THE SPINDLES"

Below: An Oldham Corporation double-decker bus makes its way up Manchester Street towards Market Place in this scene from the 1960s. The Regent Hotel is shown on the left of the photograph. The changes which had taken place in the Market Place area over a period of around half a century altered the character of the neighbourhood. The creation of the Spindles Shopping Centre has assured the importance of Market Place to the retail heart of the town. Just right of centre in this view the Market Place Post Office is visible with *Crooks* and the Prince William Hotel to the right of it.

A busy Saturday afternoon along High Street in the 1940s was recorded for us by the photographer who captured this scene. One clue to the date of the picture can be found in the poster displayed above the shop on the left, in the middle-distance. "Buy Defence Bonds!" it proclaimed. At least two of the motorcars in the picture had their headlights blacked out. Open-topped cars and shaded shop windows suggest a summertime setting and the three Manchester Corporation buses were kept busy collecting shoppers from the busy street and taking them home. We noticed the large box-van moving towards the camera. It was part of the Northumbrian Transport Services company fleet and was a long way from home on the relatively poor roads of the 1940s.

Below: Once the focus of retailing activity in Oldham, the High Street is seen here on a busy shopping day in the 1950s. Addison & Co. Ltd was a wines and spirit merchants and is featured on the left of the picture. Throughout most, if not all of the time covered by the book it would have been quite unusual for 'ordinary' folk to drink alcohol at home, other than at Christmas or other special occasions. Wines and spirits could be bought from many chemists, and a small number of merchants like *Addisons.* The consumption of alcohol was still dominated by the pub-trade. At one time in the middle of the last century, there were 250 public houses in the Oldham area for the town's 60,000 population - a massive proportion of one pub for every 240 people, and one which has never since been experienced in the area. Across the road *Boots* and the *Co-op* self-service store could be found. Boots first began trading in Oldham in 1912. Nearby Peter Street was transformed in the late 1960s by the construction of St. Peter's Precinct. This venture into the modern shopping age was not as successful as some others that have been made since, and the complex has since been superseded by the Spindles Shopping Centre.

"AT ONE TIME, THERE WERE NO FEWER THAN 250 PUBLIC HOUSES IN OLDHAM, ONE FOR EVERY 240 PEOPLE"

Above: This photograph shows the changing face of Market Street, Shaw and dates from about 1964. The shop premises on the left of the picture have taken on the bland, concrete and aluminium appearance that characterised retail properties from this time onwards, even in the smaller towns and suburbs of the district.

The very small branch of *Woolworths* is shown here - the third shop from the left, with a shiny coachbuilt pram parked on the street outside. Some of the prices from over 30 years ago can be seen on the posters in the supermarket window. We could be forgiven for being envious at how affordable things seemed by today's standards: Quash orange drink at 1s 11d, butter at 3s 11d, dog food for 1s 3d per can and rice pudding at 9d per tin.

Of course, this good value is merely an illusion as we have to remember that few people earned more that £20 per week in these days. The *Ford Corsair* seen approaching the camera from the right is worth a mention. The medium-sized saloon was available in family or 'executive' trim with engines up to two litres in capacity. Once under way they were quiet and comfortable, but many former owners may remember that they could be very reluctant to start at the slightest hint of dampness on a chilly autumn day.

Above: How things change in the space of a few years! And we don't just mean the buildings and fabric of the town, just look at the ACDO slogan "Keep Clothes Gay The ACDO Way" - this would be sure to raise an eyebrow or two if it were used in a modern setting! The picture features Royton, with Sandy Lane in the foreground. The junction with Middleton Road is just out of picture on the left. Approaching the camera is an early 1960s Wolseley 1660. This was the luxury version of the popular Austin Cambridge and Morris Oxford, complete with leather seats, wood veneer finish on the dashboard and a tuned, slightly more powerful version of the cheaper models' B.M.C engine.

Below: Changing times are depicted in this picture which dates from May 1970. Chapel Street can be seen on the left, and this corner spot was the location of Alexandre the popular tailoring establishment for many years. Alexandre's, like Burtons had a branch in virtually every town of any note and were well known for their high standards of quality and value. The sign in their window reads "order your suit for Wakes now." The period running up to Wakes Week would have been a busy one for tailors in the area because of the large number of weddings which took place at that time. A crane can be seen in the distance, part of the plant used to construct the new shop and high street bank building on the High Street. In front of that building a Hillman Superminx dating from the mid-1960s is parked.

Bird's eye view

Market trading can be seen in full swing in this picture which was taken from an altitude of 1500 feet. The almost map-like scene gives the best impression of just how extensive Oldham's market area was - and how well-supported it was too. Bargain hunters were attracted to Oldham's market stalls from far and wide, drawn by the reputation for keen prices, fresh produce and an extensive choice of everything from clothes to lightbulbs. Market trading in Oldham can be traced back at least as far as Medieval times but the town's first organised market place was set up around Church Terrace in 1817. The area became known as New Market Place. 'Tommyfield' was the solution, an area of land at the rear of the present High Street where once apple trees and fruit of various kinds was grown. As the years went by Tommy's Orchard became Tommy's Field. The Tommyfield Market covered an area of just less than 4 acres and incorporated fairground rides and various attractions to draw the crowds all year round.

"THE NEW
BY-PASS
ALLEVIATED
MUCH OF THE
PRESSURE ON
THE TOWN
CENTRE
STREETS"

Changes were well under way in the centre of Oldham when this picture was taken. The new by-pass can be seen sweeping up from the bottom left-hand corner of the photograph, past the huge circular overhead junction to the top right. In doing so the new road would serve to alleviate much of the pressure on the over-used town centre streets by separating 'through' traffic from the cars and trucks which wanted to access the centre of Oldham. The ill-fated St. Peter's Precinct can be seen under construction on the left of the picture. It would later be swept away and replaced by the successful Spindles development. Mumps railway station is visible at the top left of the picture and Union Street dissects the photograph with a diagonal course through the middle of the town.

Above: Werneth Park dominates the right hand side of this photograph with the broad-leaved trees and curved pathways making a very distinctive outline from the sky. The tropical plant house, or Arberetum can be seen beside Manchester Road on the edge of the park, Manchester Road being the long, straight route taking traffic from roughly the centre of the view at the bottom to the top right hand corner. Keen eyes may just be able to make out the outline of Hulme Grammar School on the left of Manchester Road at the top of the picture. Werneth Cricket Club can be seen on the top left of the scene and it is interesting to see how the suburban streets in the picture are laid out in a very distinctive grid pattern.

Below: A variety of sporting activities is represented in this photograph from the 1960s. Oldham Cricket Ground can be seen at the bottom of the picture to the left of the Derker district. At the left hand corner of the photograph the distinctive factory roof of the *Slumberland* works is shown, and above that, running from left to right across the picture is Ripponden Road. Slightly higher than the centre of the picture the Watersheddings Ground of Oldham Rugby League Club can be seen, and to the left of that we see the Greyhound Track. Both of these facilities have since been pulled down. The built up area shown at the top of the picture is Watersheddings.

Below: This very industrial scene from the 1950s contains a wealth of information that will be of interest to the modern reader. The area at the bottom of the picture is known as Coldhurst and contains rows of terraced houses which would have been largely occupied by workers in the surrounding mills and factories. Right in the centre of the photograph Oldham and District General Hospital can be seen; local people would have referred to it as *Boundary Park Hospital.* The establishment brought fame to Oldham when work carried on there by Mr. Patrick Steptoe resulted in the birth of the first 'test-tube' baby, Louise Brown. The hospital has since been developed and goes under the name of Royal Oldham Hospital after the closure of the Royal Infirmary. It is now one of the largest hospitals in Britain. The top right of the picture shows the Broadway area and Monarch Mill. On the left is Boundary Park, the home of Oldham Athletic Football Club, behind which is land which went on to become the Clayton playing fields. Below Boundary Park is the land which went on to be the location of Oldham running track, adjacent to Westwood Park.

"OLD ROYTON STATION WAS THE SCENE OF A WELL KNOWN TRAIN CRASH, WHEN AN ENGINE PLOUGHED THROUGH THE STATION BUFFERS AND ACROSS THE STREET IN THE LATE 1950s"

Above: An aerial view of Royton is afforded by this excellent photograph. Right in the centre of the picture is the area which went on to be developed as Royton Shopping Centre. The main road which dissects the photograph from the bottom left to the top right is Rochdale Road leading, at the top of the picture, to the Shaw Road End area in the vicinity of St. Anne's School. Just in view, beneath St. Anne's, is Delta Mill, with land in front of it which is now the site of Our Lady's Catholic School. The top left 'quarter' of the picture is dominated by Old Royton Station, the scene of a well known train crash around four decades ago. The engine crashed through the buffers in the station and travelled out of control across the road into the houses beyond. Nearer the camera, beneath the location of the Railway Station is Royton Park which stands on the left of Rochdale Road. The area at the bottom of the view has since been developed to create the Thorp Farm housing estate.

In the front line

OLDHAM EVENING CHRONICLE

Left: Putting on a brave face in the aftermath of the worst bombing raid on Oldham in the Second World War. Everything was scarce and food was especially precious; it had to be carefully salvaged at times like this. This was the scene along Green Lane, Garden Suburb on October 12th, 1941. In all 27 people died during the air raid which began at 11.00 pm lasted for two hours. Bombs fell at Foxdenton Lane, Broadway, Hollinwood Cemetery, Hollins Estate, Incline Road, Garden Suburb, Manley Road, Mirfield Avenue, Cranberry Street, Napier Street East, Leesbrook and Werneth Hall Road. throughout the Second World War there were over 300 siren alerts in Oldham and, in all, 3500 houses sustained bomb damage.

Above: This picture dates from 1942 and features six lovely young ladies, all workers in the Cotton Industry through which Oldham had become wealthy and famous. 'Cotton in the Front Line' was the slogan in the background, reminding people, if that were necessary, of the importance of the clothing and textile industries to the overall campaign against the Nazis.

Many people have fond memories of some aspects of civilian life in wartime, despite the shortages and the loss of friends and family in the conflict. From the outset there was virtually no unemployment and 'good money' could be earned at a wide range of workplaces. Women found their prospects greatly enhanced, with more chances of obtaining responsible employment immediately available. There was a real sense of purpose among the war workers and many friendships formed during those years would endure for several decades.

OLDHAM EVENING CHRONICLE

Above: This rather 'posed' photograph shows some of the staff at one of Oldham's Fire Control Centres in the early 1940s. The threat of widespread fire damage was a real one. It was taken very seriously when the preparations for civil defence were made during the Second War. The Borough's normal resource of three fire stations was increased to 16 and 120 new devices, including several fire appliances were acquired for any forthcoming inferno. Some of the staff were engaged on a voluntary basis while others were employed at £3 per week for unlimited hours (with no overtime pay), such was the fear of fire caused by enemy bombs at the time.

Above right: A stirring sight as the Home Guard marches up the incline at Rhodes Bank on 22nd May 1944. In Oldham there were no fewer than 53 basement air raid shelters (usually under shop premises) during the war and 74 communal shelters holding around 50 people each at various locations. Advertising hoardings around the town were set up to let people know where the nearest shelter was and police cars would patrol the streets with loudspeaker announcements to reinforce the

message. Dean's was the place to buy your Dunlop rain coat and even smarter clothes could be obtained from Dunn and Co. the tailors just a few doors further down the slope. 'Utility Furniture' was available at from Oldham Furnishing Ltd, which was located next to Mr. Stuttards' tobacconists' shop.

Right: Despite the wet weather the people of Oldham turned out in force to witness the ceremony which marked the official adoption of the 41st Oldham Tank Regiment by the Borough. The event took place in July 1954, some four months after a vote by Oldham Councillors confirmed that the association should be formed. Other memorable events from 1954 included the sale, by auction, of the Theatre Royal for £3,000 and the marriage of Oldham's favourite actress Dora Bryan to Bill Lawton at St. Thomas's Church, Werneth on February 7th. Government statistics revealed that 10,000 local people were on *National Assistance* and concern was expressed by the local Chief Constable about the level of accidents on the streets of Oldham when the annual death toll reached double figures.

OLDHAM EVENING CHRONICLE

OLDHAM EVENING CHRONICLE

> **"DURING WARTIME, THERE WERE 18 SIRENS AROUND THE TOWN, INCLUDING ONE LARGE ELECTRICAL DEVICE"**

Above: Curious householders and a lone police officer watch the Civil Defence Volunteers erect a temporary water pipeline across their street. An olive green *C.D* Bedford truck (similar to the *Green Goddess* auxiliary fire engines occasionally wheeled out in firemen's strikes) carrying a load of pipes can be seen in the background. The exercise was clearly intended to enable the volunteers to ensure water supplies to an area in the event of an interruption caused by wartime or natural disaster. Repair Squads also 'stood-by' for the gas, electricity and sewer systems at this time. The picture dates from 1960 and the twin towers of the Werneth Mill complex can be seen in the background.

Below: A joint A.R.P (the letters stand for 'Air Raid Precautions') and Home Guard exercise is featured in this picture which dates from around 1942. Bemused children stand in line to watch the 'casualties' as they are evacuated by ambulance by the willing volunteers. The extent of the preparations for the hostilities on the home front was impressive. Emergency Organising Committees were established in 1939 and a training school at 'Westlands' on Grange Avenue was set up to instruct all kinds of civilian volunteers. There were 18 sirens around the town, including one large electric version. They were manned continuously after the start of the war. The size of the wartime Volunteer Defence Force was equally impressive - around 6000 civilians took on the responsibility for air raid warnings, ambulance services, auxiliary first aid and fire fighters along with anti-gas crews and associated helpers. The Council purchased 40 secondhand cars to act as emergency ambulances after encountering 'some resistance' from members of the public concerning the issue of requisitioning private cars.

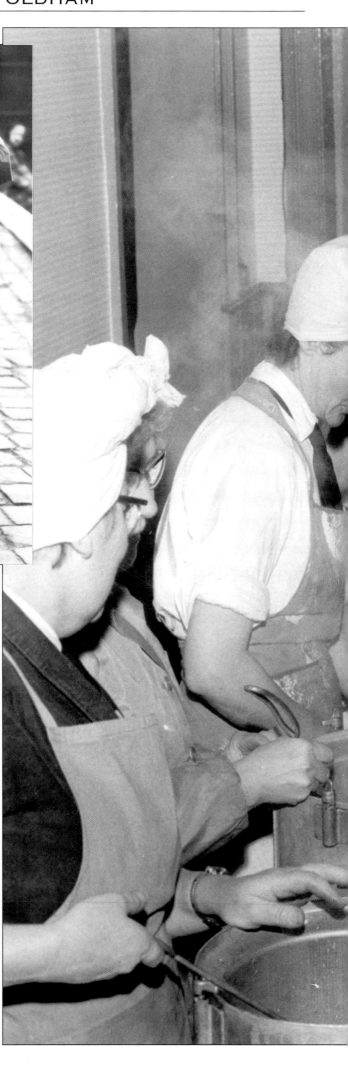

Above: More than a hint of irony here as two little innocents come face to face with an object of extreme destruction. Precious little is known about this picture, save that it was probably used as a 'promotional tool' during the Second War to motivate local people in some public appeal. There were designated weeks such as 'War Weapons Week', 'Tank Week' and 'Battle of Britain Week' which were all heavily publicised in the local press. Understandably there was a considerable amount of competition between rival towns during these campaign weeks, each of which would invariably end with the receipt of a 'thank you' letter from Winston Churchill or another senior member of the government.

Right: 'Exercise Three Owls' is depicted in this picture from October 1962. All the people featured here were members of the Civil Defence Corps, though their responsibilities were many and various. In 1953 the recruitment drive centred on the Palladium Cinema. Two films were shown there to curious audiences; *Time Bomb*, and *In Jeopardy* each designed to alert members of the public to the threat of civil disruption caused by the possibility of a nuclear attack. At the peak of its popularity the Oldham Civil Defence Corps had a membership of around 800 people - about 7 staff out of every 1,000 members of the population.

Below: It may be difficult for some younger readers to appreciate the full extent of the preparations which were in place between the late 1930s and the 1960s designed to safeguard the civilian population in the event of a national emergency. The Civil Defence organisation was a 'behind the scenes' service of ordinary men and women. They gave up some of their free time in order to undergo training which would enable them to provide emergency assistance of all kinds should the normal infrastructure we take for granted be interrupted. The creation and maintenance of the service was motivated by fear of a nuclear attack and the *cold war* that quietly raged between east and west after the end of the Second World War. These ladies were members of the County Borough of Oldham Mobile Catering Unit; they are seen here about to load their latest offerings on to the vehicle.

> **"THE CREATION OF THE C.D.C. WAS MOTIVATED BY FEAR OF A NUCLEAR ATTACK AND THE 'COLD WAR' WHICH QUIETLY RAGED BETWEEN EAST AND WEST"**

Above: *Practice makes perfect* as they say. These members of Oldham's Civil Defence Corps are seen on an exercise in the town sporting a variety of mock injuries to test the bandage-application skills of their colleagues. In the background a mobile outside catering team supplies the tea and hot food that would have kept the casualties going had there been a real emergency.

People joined the Civil Defence Corps (C.D.C.) for a variety of reasons, but one of them was certainly the social side, which was a big draw for people wanting to make new friends and share a common interest with people of a variety of ages. Recruits of the C.D.C. were expected to commit one hour per week - which could be at virtually any time to suit them, and there was no commitment required relating to the length of service necessary. The volunteers featured in these photographs would seem to confirm that view. As part of their regular training, members of the Civil Defence Corps would take part in exercises to test their various skills in the field. These pictures record the construction of a field oven made from a few dustbins and a couple of hundred bricks, working from Ministry of War plans. The people in this series of three pictures are doing a creditable job with the brickwork, laying them in battlefield conditions. The picture top left shows the early stages of the kiln

whilst the lower picture illustrates the rapid progress taking place against a backdrop of other C.D.C. members busily carrying out their own tasks. Shortly after they were built , the ovens were put to good use feeding the rest of the troops.

Along with the many social benefits the C.D.C offered there were well-known examples of the organisation assisting in civilian disasters. The best-known of these was the Harrow Rail disaster in 1952 when 112 people died and over 200 were injured. Some people argued that the reality of a nuclear war was such that the efforts of the C.D.C would be useless. Speaking in the 1950s Oldham's Assistant Regional C.D.C Officer said "statistics show that, with an effective civil defence organisation the casualties in Japan, where atom bombs were dropped, would have been reduced by 90%. Therefore the need for the present preparations is greater than ever."

On the move

Below: Oldham's Wakes holiday was the highlight of the year for many people. It was saved-up for through scores of workplace savings clubs during the year, and families would draw their Wakes Club with the hope of setting off to the coast on holiday. Blackpool, of course, was a favourite destination for Oldhamers. Families would often spend their weeks' holiday with the same landlady at the coast and it was normal to meet friends and neighbours from Oldham who were enjoying their holiday at the resort during the same week. In the days before car ownership became commonplace it was usual to travel to the coast by train. During Wakes Week scores of special trains would depart from the area's four principal stations, Werneth, Central, Hollinwood and Mumps. This picture dates from 1954 and features several very smartly dressed families about to set out on their Wakes holiday.

> "DURING WAKES WEEK, SCORES OF SPECIAL TRAINS SET OFF TO THE COAST FROM OLDHAM'S FOUR RAILWAY STATIONS"

Above: Where are they now, we wonder? This charming family scene captures the sense of excitement that accompanied a trip away to the seaside which the fortunate in Oldham could look forward to every year. Use of a magnifying glass reveals that the destination marked on the suitcases appears to be 'Middleton Towers Holiday Camp.' Everyone looks very smartly turned-out in the picture, suitcases neatly strapped up for added peace of mind. The scene dates from 1954 and keen observers may notice the distinctive outline of the Parish Church tower in the background.

Above: There are few sights involving man-made machines which are quite as awe-inspiring as the huge dark outline of a locomotive surrounded by escaping steam and bearing down on the hard steel of her thin, straight rails. The scene is given added interest by the thin covering of snow which affected this stretch of the Werneth Incline. The picture was taken to record a days' outing of a group of railway enthusiasts who were determined to travel along this section of the Werneth Incline before the rails were torn up. The letters L.C.G.B on the front of the locomotive indicate that this was a special train being run by the *Loco Club of Great Britain.*

Left: Oldham Corporation was responsible for running local bus services until October 1969 when SELNEC, later to become Greater Manchester Transport, took over. The main subject of this High Street picture is an Oldham Corporation Leyland Titan PD2/12 double decker which was purchased new in 1952. The first public bus services in Oldham began in 1913 after Oldham Tramways purchased three petrol-engined vehicles to run alongside their tramcar services. At the end of the tram era over 81 million passenger miles had been travelled by this mode of transport by a staggering 982, 941, 978 passengers. By 1962 Oldham Corporation was operating 233 buses, by now virtually all powered by diesel engines. This total was almost double the highest number of tramcars (122) operated by the Corporation at the peak of the tram age during the late 1920s.

Below: This view of Yorkshire Street, looking up from Mumps was captured in the 1950s. It is virtually impossible to look at the three coaches in the picture and not be reminded of day trips to the coast on the wallowing friendly vehicles. The distinctive aroma of stale tobacco smoke, and the heavy duty seat upholstery, especially on damp days, is something former passengers will always remember. This coach company had an office a little further along the street from where excursions could be booked. This photograph of Yorkshire Street is particularly quiet and relatively traffic free. For most of the time around the period in question it was an Oldham bottleneck capable of testing the patience of the most even-tempered traveller.

Aviation milestones from Avro to British Aerospace

The Chadderton factory's history can be traced back to the earliest days of aviation when one of the pioneers, Alliott Verdon Roe, became the first Englishman to make a powered flight. This historic event took place at the Brooklands motor racing track on June 8th 1908. Roe's flimsy machine lifted off the ground to fly just 75 feet!

This was not considered worthy of recognition, so Alliott (later Sir Alliott) was never officially credited as the first Englishman to fly. However, no-one can dispute his later claim to be the first Englishman to fly in a British aeroplane powered by a British engine. This he accomplished in July 1909 at Lea Marshes, London in his Avroplane.

After many encouraging flights, Roe decided to form his own aeroplane manufacturing company and, with financial help from his brother Humphrey, A V Roe & Company was formed in January 1910. The company was formed with the intention of using some spare space in Humphrey's surgical webbing factory at Ancoats but orders came in steadily and the production of woodwork and spares was moved to new premises in Clifton Street, Miles Platting. The firm adopted Avro as its trade name and became a limited company in 1913.

New factory announced
It was not until the beginning of the First World War that Avro began to expand. Until then it had

been just a small factory in the Manchester area but the company grew with the introduction of the Avro 504 training aeroplane. It was a great success and the type became a standard trainer for the Royal Flying Corps and, later, the fledgling Royal Air Force.

The great demand for the aircraft meant that Avro had to find new, larger premises. At first, larger floor space was found at the Park Works at Newton Heath. This factory was an extensive new engineering works built by Mather & Platt after the textile firm had diversified into electrical equipment. Three bays of the site were taken over by Avro during the First World War. Later, a purpose designed aeroplane works at Newton Heath was built for the company on Ten Acres Lane, beginning in 1918 and completed in 1920. The factory's main use had been for the production of car bodies for Crossley Motors until orders for new aircraft started to arrive again

The Newton Heath factory served Avro well during the twenties and thirties,

producing many famous aircraft such as Avian, Cadet, Tutor and Anson. However, in odd quiet moments, Avro even produced billiard tables and these are much sought after as collectors' items today.

In 1938 when war was imminent, Sir Kingsley Wood, the Air Minister, flew to Woodford Aerodrome for a visit to the Avro works. He was welcomed by Mr Roy Dobson, the Managing Director for Avro's. After an inspection of the works and a meeting with departmental heads, he announced that Avro would build a large

Above: This picture, dating from the late 1940s shows workers at the Chadderton factory inspecting Tudor airliner noses. The Tudor aircraft was not the success it should have been because the ministry of Supply insisted that the company use as many sections of the Avro Lincoln bombers as possible.

Left: Practically every square foot of floor space was taken up with the production of Lancaster bombers in this June 1944 picture. Over 3,000 Lancasters were built at Chadderton during the war. The Lancaster is remembered fondly by many as the finest bomber of World War Two.

new factory. The site chosen was alongside Greengate, in Chadderton, near Oldham. Roy Dobson, Avro's managing director and Roy Chadwick, the chief designer decided that the plant should be twice the size of other aircraft factories.

Employees from Newton Heath began moving into the new works in the Spring of 1939. First came office staff, together with workers from the Tool Room, Pattern Shop, Plating Shop and the Machine Shop. Many of them still vividly remember the move as they would be working at their benches when a tap on the shoulder and a quick 'Get your coat on!' would mean it was their turn to be transferred.

If they used a vice they were allowed to ride up to Chadderton on one of the many flatbed lorries that was moving material. Otherwise they travelled so far by bus and had to walk the rest of the way as no route went past the factory at that time.

Life was grim for a while. Workers had lacquered benches and new equipment but there were no heating or canteen facilities. Until the building was finally finished, some workers had only tarpaulin sheeting to keep off the rain.

Right: The design office at Chadderton in the 1950s where 450 draughtsmen were kept busy working on the aircraft.
Below: Chadderton was hit by a series of fires in the late 1950s. The most serious was in 1959 when a fire destroyed the Technical Library with its thousands of reference books and full records of every aircraft built by Avro. The next morning the workers saw a dreadful sight with roofless buildings and blackened walls

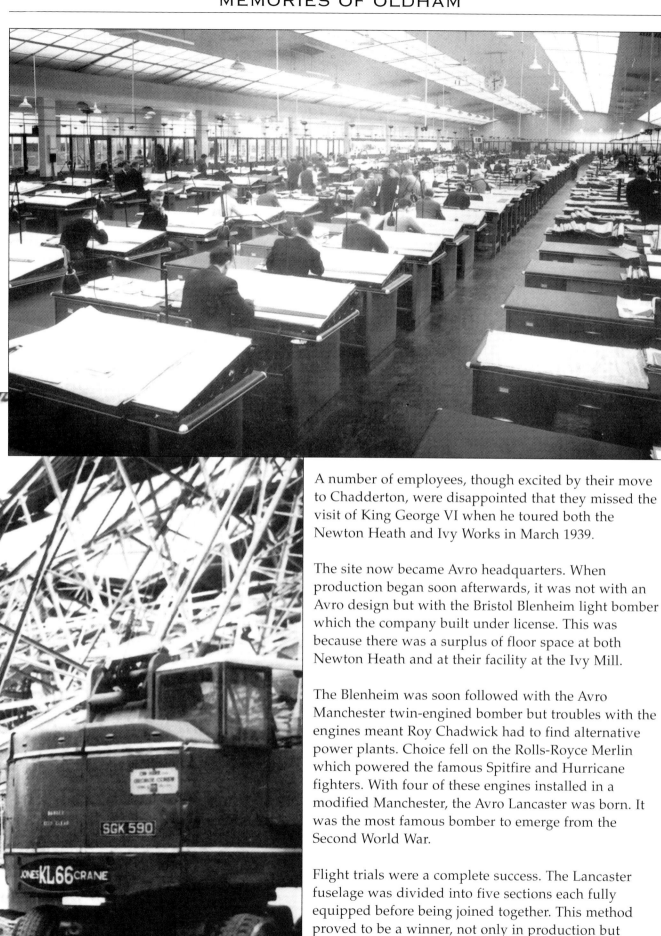

A number of employees, though excited by their move to Chadderton, were disappointed that they missed the visit of King George VI when he toured both the Newton Heath and Ivy Works in March 1939.

The site now became Avro headquarters. When production began soon afterwards, it was not with an Avro design but with the Bristol Blenheim light bomber which the company built under license. This was because there was a surplus of floor space at both Newton Heath and at their facility at the Ivy Mill.

The Blenheim was soon followed with the Avro Manchester twin-engined bomber but troubles with the engines meant Roy Chadwick had to find alternative power plants. Choice fell on the Rolls-Royce Merlin which powered the famous Spitfire and Hurricane fighters. With four of these engines installed in a modified Manchester, the Avro Lancaster was born. It was the most famous bomber to emerge from the Second World War.

Flight trials were a complete success. The Lancaster fuselage was divided into five sections each fully equipped before being joined together. This method proved to be a winner, not only in production but during operations when battle-damaged sections could easily be replaced by new ones.

Roy Dobson decided that the high production targets could be achieved by using mainly semi-skilled labour and large numbers of both men and women were

recruited. As the effort built up employees worked for 12 hour days, with seven days working and an average 66 hour week being normal. Some workers were given halibut liver oil capsules to keep them fit.

When one worker demanded a rise for working such long hours, Roy Dobson pointed out his bed in an adjoining room and explained that his own working day was 24 hours. Air raids constantly interrupted work. One night early on in the hostilities the siren sounded 27 times. Sometimes, after one of these long shifts the workers had to walk home because the air raids had stopped all transport.

Vital equipment was protected from blast damage by thick brick walls. Once, a bomb hit the rivet store sending millions of rivets in all directions. Later, blind workers sorted them by feel!

However, morale was never a problem. Workers knew they were building the RAF's greatest bomber.

During that war, 7,000 Lancasters were produced, almost half of these being produced at Chadderton, the remainder being made at other Avro sites or under license by a number of aircraft companies.

Peacetime and new designs

Many new aircraft were introduced by the Chadderton design team. One of the two most famous was the Avro-Shackleton maritime reconnaissance aircraft which served with the RAF for over 40 years. The other was the mighty Vulcan delta-winged jet bomber which became the backbone of Britain's nuclear deterrent force.

In 1951 a gentleman named Albert Platt retired from the Estimating Department at Chadderton. He was 75 years old and had started work at Brownsfield Mill in December 1909, helping Alliott Verdon Roe to establish his factory a month before the company was formed.

In 1951 Chadderton made another break from Avro designs when the Ministry asked the Company to build a batch of English Electric Canberra twin-jet bombers. Not long afterwards it also gave the go-ahead for the newly designed Avro 720, a rocket-powered interceptor. Unfortunately, when this was in an advanced stage in the Experimental Department, the project was cancelled as an economy measure.

On November 8th 1955 HRH, the Duke of Edinburgh, an enthusiastic aviator, visited over 30 departments at Chadderton, lingering in many until he was considerably behind schedule.

In 1957, when Duncan Sandys announced that there would be no more manned bombers in the RAF, work was concentrated on the Avro 748, a 44-seat civil airliner.

Fires, but business as usual

During 1959, 60 and 61 the factory was hit by a series of fires. The most serious was in 1959 when a fire destroyed the Technical Library with its thousands of reference books and full records of every aircraft built by Avro. The next morning the workers saw a dreadful sight with roofless buildings and blackened walls which must have reminded them of the Blitz. Fortunately the main Vulcan production line escaped serious damage. Tremendous efforts were made and in four months most of the staff were back in their refurbished offices. A later fire destroyed the Experimental Department and yet another the Accounts Offices.

Change of name

After the war, Avro's title was absorbed into Hawker-Siddeley Aviation with the industry's rationalisation in 1963. After further changes in 1977, the Chadderton plant became part of British Aerospace.

Recent aircraft produced at Chadderton include the Avro 748 and ATP Advanced Turboprop airliners. Components are made for the BAe 146 and RJ Regional Jet Avroliner. The latter are not so familiar as their predecessors but they are no less significant in the world air transport industry. Chadderton also produces major components for all the series of the highly successful European Airbus. A large order book has kept the factory busy.

Chadderton forms an important part of British Aerospace and the Company is currently investing heavily in high-technology, high-volume production equipment. This investment is aimed at on-going programmes such as the ever-growing workload on the Airbus series of aircraft.

In the early 1990s, Chadderton and Woodford were separated to become independent units with a high degree of responsibility for their own destiny. Consequently, for the first time, Chadderton could actively seek work from other companies. They therefore brought in work from other aerospace companies worldwide.

In January 1995 British Aerospace formed a new company to look after its manufacturing efforts. As a result, Chadderton became a key site in British Aerospace Aerostructures Limited. With around 1,800 personnel, the British Aerospace site on Greengate is the largest employer in the area and the site is well known to the residents of the surrounding towns of Oldham, Middleton, Rochdale and Manchester.

In early 1997, the Chadderton Site became part of British Aerospace Military Aircraft and Aerostructures, which covers seven sites nationwide and employs up to 20,000 people.

Today, work at Chadderton includes Airbus and RJ components, along with third party work from North American airline companies.

Chadderton has been able to secure this work by being flexible and cost effective in today's competitive marketplace.

To celebrate its proud heritage the site has opened its own Heritage & Visitors Centre. This is open to schools and the general public on a pre-booked basis and includes a slide presentation and factory tour. For bookings telephone 0161 681 2020.

Facing page: The construction of Vulcan nose sections in the late 1950s.
Below: The Avro 720 jet and rocket powered interceptor fighter in Chadderton's experimental department in 1956. This aircraft was in an advanced stage of completion when it's 'plug was pulled' due to governmental economy cuts.

The company that began with one man's dream

The origins of the Oldham Motor Company began in 1907. The man with the idea was Ralph Rothwell Eglin who had a bicycle shop on Yorkshire Street. He specialised in retailing locally made bicycles, amongst which was Rothwells.

His wife, Ada sold cigarettes and sweets on the opposite side of the road. To maintain his cycle shop he did quite an amount of bike racing in the local area as he was an enthusiastic cycler, as well as teaching people the rudiments of cycling in the comfort of a closed hall during the winter months.

At about this time, Rothwells had begun to make motor cars and Ralph was keen to get into this line of business. He approached a group of friends and acquaintances he had met through his business and arranged a meeting to discuss his idea. They met on 21st November 1907 at the offices of one of the men in Bow Street, behind Yorkshire Street. There were seven men altogether, from butchers to confectioners and rope manufacturers.

All listened to Ralph with avid interest and it was agreed that a company

would be formed in order to sell the new motor cars. With a capital of £5,000 in £1 shares, Oldham Motor Company was born on 12th December 1907, with Ralph as secretary. The business took off almost straight away when in January the company signed agencies for Argyle and Rover cars, as well as for Shell Spirit. The first vehicle that was sold was an Argyle.

Above: The service department from the 1950s.
Top left: An early advertisement for Ford vehicles, this one for the Touring Car at a cost of £128, roughly a hundred weeks' wages at the time.
Left: The premises on Manchester road.
Right: Inside the Manchester Road showrooms in the 1950s.

More agencies were taken on in the first two years, including Rothwell and Eclipse MFG.

The original home of the company was Hardings Carriage works at the corner of Manchester Road and Oxford Street which were acquired at a yearly rent of £80. The company retained the original premises until 1927 when the lease expired.

Ralph's second child was born in 1911 which turned out to be an eventful year for him as later a move to another location on Manchester Road occurred when it took on the Ford dealership and became the thirteenth Ford dealer to be appointed in the UK in October 1911.

It became obvious that another avenue of profit was the repair and supply of parts for the vehicles they sold and the firm arranged for Clincher and Continental Tyres to be supplied on a sale or return basis. In the first six months the firm made a profit of £103 16 7d.

The new premises were brighter and more modern. Huge windows allowed for better displays and more showroom area meant more cars could be shown. However in the first year of

business at these premises the company sold just ten cars. It is hardly surprising considering the times and the fact that a Ford van would set you back £120. An average week's wages was £1.20. But by the end of 1912 there were 25 staff on the books, which is fairly conclusive proof that the Ford franchise, coveted in any town had finally worked.

The showrooms and workshops purchased in readiness for the Ford franchise have since been demolished for road widening which took place in 1992/1993.

The business was passed down through the Eglin family, from father to son. Ralph's son (Ralph Jnr.) took over on Ralph's death and then his two sons, Tony and Robin joined the business. The fourth generation of the family, Robin's son, Jonathan is now working in the business.

On taking on the Ford franchise in 1911, the other franchises were transferred to the Paragon Motor Company in Oldham. In 1979 the company purchased a garage in Chorley, about an hour's drive away and this became an extension of the firm, being a Ford dealer in its own right. This company now trades as OMC Ford Chorley.

Robin Eglin, the current managing director and grandson of the founder has a right to be proud of his ancestry. Ralph Eglin worked hard for his dream and it would be beyond even his wildest dreams to see his achievements now.

The Oldham Motor Company has been a part of the town's culture for almost a century and these days when haste is of the essence this company can offer a good, old fashioned service with traditional values. Having said that, however, The Oldham Motor Company offers the latest in computerised technology and service equipment, having spent £150,000 in 1997 on bodyshop and workshop equipment. It was with a past that was full of hope and ambition that the present was formed, and with the family's desire to expand and adapt to changing needs the future looks bright for the company.

Above: A 1960s view of the Manchester Road premises with an impressive line up of Cortina MK1 cars catching the eye of one gentleman.
Facing page, bottom: On the right of Manchester Road are the old showrooms. On the left is the new 4.5 acre site prior to current development (which cost over £1 million).
Facing page, top: The parts department in the 1950s.

Outskirts

Below: A picture dating from 1949, taken during a lull in the traffic to record the appearance of the newly resurfaced road. The public house on the right of the picture is the Duke of York which was situated at 64 Rochdale Road Royton. Note the very ornate lamp standard positioned quite close to each other along the road. They also serve to carry four telephone wires on each side of the poles along this busy route.

Right: The clarity of this picture belies the fact that it is almost a century old. It was taken in the reign of Edward VII in 1909, just a year before the King died and was succeeded by George V. The hats and coats worn by the ladies in the photograph are unmistakably Edwardian in style. We can detect the limitations of the photographers' art at this time - note how most of the children look slightly blurred in the picture, obviously because they had been moving while the film was exposed, despite strict instructions to keep still for twenty seconds or so. Remarkably, some of the older people in the scene would have been born in the 1850s!

The photograph was taken to record the planting of trees at Garden Suburb.

Below right: A very tranquil view of the Garden Suburb in the summer of 1909 was captured by the photographer in this picture. The scene reminds us of some of the early British films and is given added character by the neat gardens, picket fences and the delightful gas lamp which would have provided welcome illumination during the evenings. The scene provides a sharp contrast to the grimy, crowded housing which characterised the centre of Oldham which existed during the same era. The quality of housing had a direct effect on the health and life-expectancy of the people who lived in them, as did the proximity of the houses to the smoke-belching chimneys which served the town's industry. It would be another half a century before real progress was made towards achieving satisfactory living conditions for the vast majority of families in the town.

Above: Part of the post-war housing drive is seen in this view of the 'Scheme number 8' - the construction of blocks of housing along Vulcan Street. The site looks rather deserted and reports from this time suggested that the availability of skilled building workers was one of the (many) reasons for Oldham seemingly not keeping up with the progress made in the rest of Britain. Of 57 Local Authorities with a population of more than 100,000 people only Oldham had completed the construction of *no* permanent and *no* temporary houses by the end of August 1946. It was the worst record of any large borough in the Country, but it was one that was matched by many of the smaller borough's in Britain. Indeed, 841 of the Country's 1470 local authorities had failed to complete a single new house during the first year after the end of the war.

Above right: 'Houses fit for heroes to live in' are seen under construction here in July 1946. A national drive to improve the housing stock was under way at this time and Oldham did not initially enjoy a great deal of success with their contribution to it. This development was designated 'Scheme number 2' and was located at Moorside Avenue. Five years before this picture was taken a survey identified 9,000 unfit houses (as carefully defined by Government-supplied criteria in the 1930 Housing Act) and 2,400 of these were of the 'back-to-back' variety. In common with many other large Boroughs Oldham experimented with temporary pre-fabricated houses. An order for 50 Pre-Fabs was placed soon after this picture was taken.

Right: This evocative photograph was taken on November 5th 1946. It features 'Scheme number 2' of the Council's grand plan to improve the town's ailing housing stock in line with the national housing scheme. These houses were better known as Borrowdale Avenue on the Strinesdale Estate. In the January of the year this scene was recorded the Housing Committee voted for the disbanding of the Womens' Housing Advisory Committee and declared a new target of 3,000 new houses to be built within 3 years. Delays were experienced with the supply of materials in the years which followed the end of the Second World War and appeals were made by local Councillors and housing officials for everyone concerned to get behind the drive to build new homes. The task of rehousing the thousands of people living in unsuitable accommodation was to pre-occupy Oldham's local government for many decades.

Above: This picture was entitled "Housing conditions in Oldham" by the photographer who recorded the scene back in 1965. Of course, the setting for the picture was typical of many backstreet Oldham areas and the poor little girl was not alone, having nowhere suitable to play during her childhood. But this was not to say that every street in Oldham looked like this! A council report from 1941 highlighted the problems associated with the town's housing stock. It identified the disturbing fact that 12,500 houses were built before 1875, and that 9,000 houses were unfit for human habitation. The intervention of the war meant that little was done about the problem and by 1951 there were still 26,000 people living in houses with no separate internal accommodation. The 1951 plan set a target of 10,000 new homes to be built over the next 20 years.

Shopping spree

Below: 'Factory shops' are evidently nothing new if this picture from around 1915 is anything to go by. The photograph was taken outside Sutcliffe Mill at Shaw on a windy May Saturday during the First World War. There seem to be plenty of bargains on offer even though this is billed as 'the last day of the sale.' The two youngest girls, dressed in white, look as if they may be twins and are about 12 years old. This would have been old enough to work 'half time' in the mill and the second half of the day would be spent at school. Even the 'half timers worked long hours by today's standards - a 6.00 am start then working through until 12.30 pm. Many children would find it difficult, and sometimes impossible to stay awake during afternoon lessons. Life was incredibly arduous for most people in Oldham at the time this picture was taken, as it was for those in most industrial towns. There existed a constant battle to put food on the table and fend off the countless diseases which threatened the lives of the very young and the very old - not that it was expected for many people to live to a ripe old age without a hefty dose of good luck.

> "LIFE WAS ARDUOUS FOR MOST PEOPLE IN OLDHAM AT THE TURN OF THE CENTURY"

Below: A very natural shopping scene featuring Robinsons stall in the Victoria Market Hall. The Robinson's sold biscuits and some other groceries here until the disastrous market fire in 1974. Everyone in the picture seems very jolly but it has to be said that the establishment looks rather murky in certain areas compared with the bright modern retail units we are used to today. Remarkably, two boxes of Kellogg's cornflakes can be seen on the shelf on the left of the picture, looking almost identical to the ones on sale today. Most other aspects of food retailing have changed dramatically in the half century or so since this scene was recorded. Pre-packed foods are far more typical now, and electronic weighing scales have replaced the individual weights and sturdy scales that used to be employed. This was the era of *proper shopping* when everyone seemed to have time for a friendly word and a smile for each other - on both sides of the counter.

Above: Hardcastles were noted for their fine ladies clothing and their window display shown here has managed to cram all manner of goods into the unusually tall and narrow windows. Hardcastles was founded by Mr. Christopher Hardcastle, an industrious entrepreneur from the West Midlands. Rising from humble beginnings he created the successful department store business and became a leading member of the Oldham Chamber of Commerce in later years. The offices above this part of the store were occupied by William Ellison 'Estate, Insurance and Business Agents' who specialised in selling small businesses in the area and some distance beyond. Another office above the shop was the local branch of the National Cash Register Company Ltd. Hardcastles closed in 1987.

Above: This scene was recorded in about 1963 and features, of course, Tommyfield Market. This was the era of the vinyl shopping bag, the knee-length overcoat and the ubiquitous headscarf. In the days before supermarkets were as well established as they are today the markets enjoyed greater patronage than they do in modern times. Fewer people owned cars, and for many people the weekly shopping expedition was much more of a chore than it is today, with everything being carried home on the bus. Over the last 100 years there have been many 'shopping revolutions' but market traders have continued to serve a large population with 'no-frills' fresh produce at prices that few other retailers can compete with.

"THE 60S SAW A REVOLUTION IN THE WAY THAT PEOPLE DID THEIR SHOPPING"

Below: Market Street, Shaw, at the corner of Rochdale Road, was dominated by the Electricity Services shop when this scene was captured around 40 years ago. It was the dawn of the 1960s. One of the more notable icons of the era was the large coachbuilt pram, possibly a *Silver Cross*, the Rolls Royce of their type and the apple of every expectant mother's eye. The sign marking the location of 'Vernons Pricedown' is clearly seen in the picture; they were popular grocers for many years. J. Lees and Sons were butchers next door, and beyond the narrow alley to the left of the butchers was the local chemists. The photograph was taken at the start of the 1960s, a period which would see a revolution in the way people did their shopping throughout the country.

The birth of a new shopping era

Before the arrival of the Town Square Shopping Centre most local people remember the site as a convenient car park, but in fact the area has a history dating back to the earliest days of the village of Oldham.

The original St Peter's Church was built in 1758 and was replaced in 1901 by a much larger building. The 'new' church was built over a large part of the former graveyard and when it was finally demolished in 1970, some of its stone was used in an extension on the Parish Church.

Many people will recall the Technical College on Ascroft Street. Built in 1897 as the Municipal Technical School, the college was the centre for training textile engineers for many years. There were also as many as five hotels and ten public houses in the centre, within a stone's throw of the area.

1914 saw the opening of Yate's Wine Lodge Bakery in St Peters Street, next door to Oldham Mutual Sick and Burial Society. This society was founded in the mid 1900s because of the 'dissatisfaction with the glaring extravagances of the Manchester Sick and Burial Society'.

St Peters Street, Denton Street, School Croft, Chapel Street and Parliament Street have all been relegated to history now.

The Town Square Shopping Centre was officially opened in 1981 and was built as a direct response to demand by shoppers for a newer, brighter look in Oldham.

Above: St Peters Church in February 1967. This was during the days when the area was most noted for its convenient town centre parking.
Left: A view of High Street taken in March 1970. The Town Square Shopping Centre was to take up part of the left hand side of the street.

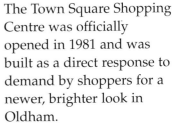

Costing £9 million, it was the first major shopping centre in the UK to be designed and constructed by one single company.

Only five months separated the signing of the contracts from the beginning of work and despite the appalling winter weather conditions of 1979, the work was done on schedule. Another 'fly in the ointment' was the actual site of the new development. The 'Oldham Fault' is a name generally given to this area, above an abandoned mine workings and the existence of a ground abnormality. Considerable investigations and tests had to be done, resulting in necessary supports being constructed. These

resemble huge stalactites, which are visible in the underground service area.

As with all things, fashions change as time goes by. By 1990 it was felt that the centre, like many of its era, had a somewhat traditional feel which didn't reflect the demands of modern shoppers. As a result, Scottish Amicable undertook a refurbishment in order for it to continue to provide a good environment in the 1990s.

The centre was well loved by the people of Oldham, and was thought to be the focus of the town's retailing activity. The refurbishment took this into account and was designed sympathetically.

The refurbishment maximised the potential of the link between Town Square Shopping Centre and the proposed new Spindles Centre, the idea being that the two run adjacent to each other, whilst maintaining their own separate identities.

The end result was satisfying. The Town Square Shopping Centre is still the hub of retailing in Oldham and will continue to be so for many years to come.

Above: *The development of the centre began in 1979. In this picture Yate's Wine Lodge is on the left. The extent of the undertaking is obvious.*
Left: *A scene from before refurbishment took place in the early 1990s......*
Below: *......and afterwards. A safe, clean and relaxed atmosphere.*

The art of shopping in the heart of Oldham

Oldham has undergone a radical transformation in the past 20 years, The dominance in the first half of the Century of the textile industry (from which The Spindles takes its name) has been replaced by a diverse manufacturing base with a strong representation of high technology industries. The town has continued this expansion even in difficult periods.

In the last decade Oldham has increased its total number of jobs by 11,000 and increased its number of businesses by 20%. The town has also developed with long term investments in infrastructure, housing and amenities, but until The Spindles, retail development had lagged behind.

The area benefits from an excellent communication network. The Greater Manchester orbital motorway system and its feeder to Oldham, the A627M, have directly influenced the towns recent growth and success. The completion of the last phase of the Manchester outer ring road, the M66, will hopefully unlock Oldham's potential even further.

Echoing the best of Oldham's past and its fine Victorian architecture, The Spindles facades are finished in a tradi-tional red brick with detailing in natural stone and slate. The focus of the scheme is a giant rotunda which is visible for many miles outside the town. Its dramatic galleried atrium houses the foodcourt above the entrances from Market Place and the bus station which lead to the escalators to the two levels of shopping malls.

The malls converge in Central Square under a further galleried atrium which opens out to the two departmental stores at the heart of The Spindles. Both atriums feature remarkable stained glass roofs designed by the internationally acclaimed artist, Brian Clarke, who was born in Oldham.

The interior design provides equal prominence and visibility to the two malls and light from the glazed roofs above the malls permeates right through the shopping centre

The lower mall features 'pop out' shop fronts while the upper mall is set back from the malls to provide maximum visibility. All the textures and colours have been chosen to complement the architecture which features steel arches and stone pillars to echo Oldham's

Victorian Market Hall which was destroyed by a fire.

The Spindles opened for trading in September 1993. There is a 950 space car park on seven levels and being linked to the recently renovated Town Square shopping centre next door, Oldham can claim to offer one of the largest covered shopping areas outside Manchester.

Within the rotunda area there is a 250 seat foodcourt with views out on to the High Street, Market Place and Cheapside and this has become a focal point for the people of Oldham. Being located at the heart of Oldham shopping in The Spindles is a major force in retailing in the town and has restored Oldham's position as the place to shop. Its corner-stone position within the town makes it the natural destination for shopping in Oldham by public and private transport.

The centre was originally developed by the Burwood House Group and was sold in December 1995 to Prudential Portfolio Managers who have already become a major force in the town of Oldham and have future plans to improve The Spindles and keep it amongst the hierarchy of shopping centres in the North West.

A unique experience and traditionally friendly welcome awaits visitors to The Spindles shopping centre and it is immediately apparent that this is one venue that really does care.

Oldham has many exciting developments in the pipeline for the future. A full town centre CCTV system is now up and running. This coupled with other developments such as the proposed extension to Town Square and the relocation of the bus station to the entrance by The Spindles' rotunda, the Arcades development on the High Street and probably most important to be seen in the future is the Union Street retail and leisure development adjacent to the proposed cultural quarter.

The Union Street development will be open in the near future with retail space, a multi-screen cinema, ten pin bowling and other leisure facilities which will hopefully have a great impact on the town. This, together with the Metrolink tram system, which will come to Oldham early in the new millennium will draw more custom into the town from the surrounding areas.

Above: The Rotunda entrance to The Spindles.
Left: An internal view of the shopping centre.
Facing page: An aerial picture showing the shopping centre in the heart of Oldham. Its sympathetic facade blends in with its surroundings and since its opening in 1993 it has proved to be an enormous success.

Two centuries of street trading

The first mention of a market in Oldham was in 1788 when butchers set up stalls at the top of George Street each Saturday night. At the end of trading the butchers would sell any meat they had left very cheaply as it would not be fit to eat by the following Monday when their shops were opened again.

Other traders then opened stalls along High Street as far as the Parish Church. Because the area became very crowded, the stallholders were eventually persuaded to move their stalls into a field behind Albion Street, which belonged to a man called Thomas Whittaker. This is the reason that the open market is still known as Tommyfield. Over the years, more and more stalls were added, until the market reached the size it is today.

There have been four Market Halls in Oldham. The first was built by a number of local shopkeepers in 1856 and was later bought by the council. In 1865, Parliament passed an act which allowed the Council to take rents from market stall holders.

In 1908 the old market was replaced with a larger new building which was named the Victoria Market

Hall. This lasted until October 1974 when it was destroyed in a huge fire so fierce that it could be seen many miles away. The heat broke shop windows on the other side of Albion Street and Henshaw Street.

Above: Inside Victoria Market in the 1960s.
Below: A view from Henshaw Street c1960s, looking towards Albion Street merging from the right.

Early in 1975 a temporary market hall was opened to replace the one that had been burnt down. This one was demolished when the new market hall was put up in the very early nineties. This one opened in 1990. It has 232 stalls and twenty shops which are modern and colourful and the hall provides a bright and pleasant place to shop.

The open market is held on Tommyfield at the rear of the market hall every Monday, Friday and Saturday. There are 300 stalls and Tommyfield is among the largest open markets in the north of England. Here you can buy almost anything - or have a ride on a roundabout as many of us did when we were younger. Every Wednesday there is a second-hand market which is very popular. Traders come from all over Lancashire and Yorkshire, even one or two from as far away as London, to sell old clothes and antiques.

There is a staff of six in the market office. Headed by David Girdlestone, they have to organise everything, from collecting the rents and letting the stalls to answering questions and offering all kinds of assistance to shoppers. Eleven other workers keep the market clean and repair the stalls and buildings.

One of them drives a tractor round the stalls early in the morning, pulling a train of boxes of goods.

At the end of trading, all the rubbish is collected and placed in three compactors that crush it before it is taken to the tip.

The rents of all the markets amount to well over a million pounds. After expenses have been paid, the profits go towards keeping down the amount of the various local taxes!

Above: Victoria Market Hall c1960s.
Left: The New Market Hall taken in April 1990.

At work

Below: A sea of faces look towards the camera in this picture taken inside the sewing room at Park Mill on Bleasdale Street. The scene dates from October 1946 and of course the vast majority of the workforce in the mill were women. There would be precious few moments like this when the nimble fingers of these young ladies were stationary long enough to have a picture taken. Their feet would have been very active too, for the sewing machines they worked on were operated by treadles, much as the domestic machines some of our mothers used were. The picture dates from a time before modern strip lights illuminated every place of work and these large 150w bulbs provided the only lighting for the ladies' needlework. Modern machinists have a small lamp fixed on the side of their work station for the best possible visibility. As a point of interest, two weeks after this picture was taken the National Health Service was launched in Britain.

Below right: There is something quite poignant about this 1930s photograph showing a young woman at work in one of Oldham's many cotton mills. She looks very vulnerable - a delicate young thing surrounded by the exposed chains and cogs of the loom she is minding. Accidents were all too common in these precarious surroundings. We can only guess where her thoughts would be for, despite the apparent concentration, she would be working on 'auto-pilot' despite all the din that characterised the mill workers' environment. Perhaps she had a young man, or even a young family to occupy her thoughts? Women like her were the 'unsung heroes' upon whom much of the wealth of the cotton industry was created..... though tradition was that they never got to see much of it.

Left: In today's environmentally conscious world it is difficult to imagine what life was like for people living in the conditions portrayed in this photograph. This picture is generally accepted to be a heavily re-touched photograph of the Oldham skyline, but despite the contrived exaggeration we know for certain that no square inch of the town escaped the muck and grime that accompanied the pollution as sure as night followed day. It was not until the 1960s that improvements really got under way, and some years after that before public buildings were cleaned of the dirt and grime which had been the unwelcome by-products of Oldham's industrial success.

Below: Long delays were experienced along Rochdale Road in 1949 when major resurfacing work was being undertaken. The road-laying equipment looks very similar to that used almost half a century later, though the headgear worn by the workmen is rather different. Berets were made popular by the war which had ended only four years before this picture was taken. It was common for *working men* to wear ex-army clothing such as battledress tunics, army boots and berets as working clothes. These may have been their own from the war or purchased from one of the many army surplus shops. On the left of the photograph a large black hearse can be seen - complete with coffin, though nobody appears to be taking any notice.

> "THE MEN IN THE SERVICES FOUGHT THE WAR BUT THE WORKERS WON IT"

Above: Some blatant but understandable wartime propaganda is featured in this photograph from 1942. Mary Stanyer, a 29-year-old Card Room worker is seen demonstrating her work in process of manufacturing of airmen's clothing. The dashing visitor to the factory was Flight Lieutenant Thomas Francis Neil D.F.C, a wartime fighter pilot of great distinction with looks that would have made the hearts of his young female admirers flutter. The young airman's motivational message to the staff at the mill was intended to spur them on to greater heights of productivity; "When this war is finished the men in the Services will have fought the war, but you will have won it."

Above: This 1950s Manchester Cotton Board picture has a medical theme and features a young lady being advised by an authoritative-looking matron. During the decade Oldham's medical needs were catered for by several institutions, including Boundary Park Hospital and Annexe (390 beds and 762 beds), Oldham Royal Infirmary (200 beds), Westhulme Isolation Hospital (86 beds), Strineside Sanatorium (57 beds) and Woodfield Nursing Home (20 beds).
In addition the Council ran 8 branch clinics and various school clinics.

"DURING THE 1950s, OLDHAM'S MEDICAL NEEDS WERE SERVED BY NO FEWER THAN SIX INSTITUTIONS"

Below: This photograph shows a young lady engaged in cone winding in one of the many Oldham cotton mills that survived into the 1960s. The population of Oldham has risen and fallen at times in line with the prosperity or otherwise of the cotton industry. In the late 1940s Oldham was the premier cotton town of the world. It was a time when well over half of Lancashire's entire annual output of cotton yarn was produced in Oldham's mills. Later years would see trade suffer from a combination of cheap foreign imports and the rise of man-made fibres. The decline resulted in the loss of many jobs and the demolition of scores of mill property that once seemed as permanent as the Pennine hills themselves.

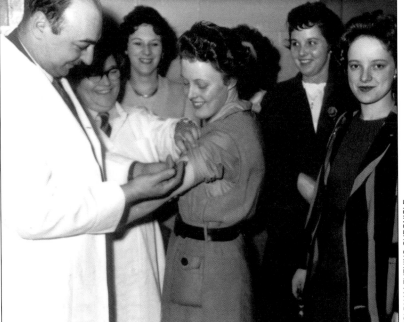

OLDHAM EVENING CHRONICLE

Above: September 1958 saw the popular political leader Hugh Gaitskill visit several mills as part of a northern fact-finding tour. He is seen here chatting to some young lady mill workers as they take their dinner break. It would appear that his fact-finding efforts didn't include eating a typical canteen lunch! 1958 contained a number of national political milestones and was the first year that Life Peers were appointed to the House of Lords. The Campaign For Nuclear Disarmament was set up in February under the presidency of Bertrand Russell. The Labour M.P Michael Foot and the writer J.B Priestley were among the first members. Christabel Pankhurst the suffragette died in March and the year saw the formation of the European Economic Community.

Above right: Tanfield Youth Centre was the venue for mass inoculations against Polio when this photo-graph was taken in 1959. There appear to be one or two nervous smiles around the room, and no wonder as vaccinations were not considered as routine as they are today. Indeed, the *Salk* polio vaccine which revolutionised the battle against the

horrible disease had only been successfully tested in the USA six years before this picture was taken. Polio was a dreaded phenomenon and epidemics were regularly reported. Smallpox was another feared affliction and vaccination was compulsory under the 1946 Health Act. Sadly, not all parents took advantage of this free protection against the disease and there were many cases of parents being fined in sittings at local courts.

SELHAL - providing homes for Oldham

SELHAL is a not for profit landlord and developer. It has been providing housing solutions for a range of people with housing needs in Oldham for thirty years. In that time, it has provided high quality, warm and secure homes for thousands of individuals and families. For most of its thirty years the principal area of its investment has been in Oldham.

The acronym 'SELHAL' has been the title by which the Housing Association has been known for all of its life. It derives from the full name of the company, the South East Lancashire Housing Association Limited. It was originally incorporated on 21st November 1967 as the Medlock Housing Society. Revised objects were incorporated on 18th March 1970 when the now familiar title was agreed by the Registrar of Industrial & Provident Societies.

SELHAL was confirmed in its status as an organisation to provide social housing, in other words, quality flats and houses at affordable rents. Lettings in its early years, to about 1981, were made to older people with housing needs. 'Needs' could mean actual or potential homelessness, it could mean living in overcrowded or unhealthy conditions. In some cases the lettings were also made to release large properties back on to the housing market. This was the circumstances of SELHAL's, second tenant, Mrs Margaret Bird, who recently passed her 25th anniversary as a tenant in the Association's first development, Edward Mews. Margaret's family had grown up and left home. She struggled at the time to maintain her house in Werneth and a first floor flat answered all of her prayers for warm and safe housing in the community she had spent most of her life in.

The vision and energy that created SELHAL is attributed to Phillip Moster. Phillip was Clerk to the Chadderton Urban District Council in the 1960s. As the senior employee of the Council, he understood better than most that whilst the council housing boom of the 1960s was building hundreds of homes each year these were going predominately to families. The housing waiting lists for flats for older people were long. They often disadvantaged applicants who had stressful circumstances because of their health or the housing conditions they lived in.

Phillip Moster assembled a powerful committee of people who understood the property and construction world. They became the founding Board members. They included Alan Lees, of Cameron Middleton Lees (Quantity Surveyors), Roger Needham of Hall Needham (Architects), Alan Powell of local contractors Partingtons, with able support from Kenneth Hirst of the Oldham Evening Chronicle and Alan Postle, Bank Manager for National Westminster Bank. The Secretary was Jack Smith of Ryder & Dutton, which provided the early home for the conduct of business. This was out of 15 Union Street.

> "SELHAL, FOUNDED IN 1967, HAS INVESTED £31 MILLION IN HOMES FOR OLDHAM."

*Above: SELHAL's, second tenant, Mrs Margaret Bird, who recently passed her 25th anniversary as a tenant in the Association's first development with Chief Executive, Mel Godfrey. **Left:** The Mayoress of Oldham at the official opening of Grange Court in Coppice.*

Since then SELHAL has worked steadily down Union Street, occupying its fourth address now at 111 Union Street - some 300 yards away.

The early ideals were to provide housing of quality that would be accessible, attractive places to live. These development ideals remain to this day.

Testimony to this is that all of the earliest housing schemes, such as Grange Court, remain popular and sought after housing as we turn into the twenty first century.

In 1974, Chadderton UDC and other local UDCs merged into a new unitary local authority, Oldham Borough Council. By the early 1980s the housing needs of Oldham were changing, aided by shifts in government grant support. Investment moved towards tackling the large number of damp, unfit and often overcrowded terraced houses that then made up a significant proportion of Oldham's housing stock. SELHAL was awarded the role of rehabilitating homes in Coppice and Werneth which in many cases had been neglected for decades by their previous landlord - owners.

In June 1980, Charles Cadbury, of the famous confectionery family, became the organisation's first Managing Director. The housing stock grew rapidly, providing flats for the older person and the disabled and houses for families. With a dedicated and energetic staff team the housing projects the organisation took on were becoming more complex, the housing needs more acute and the housing solutions

more innovative. One such example was the Malton Street area of Coppice. Two streets of terraced houses were demolished to make way for new, large family homes on land that posed formidable technical problems to the design team. Deep foundations and the construction of a gabian wall secured the construction of 43 homes whose centrepiece is the corbelling from the former Werneth Fire Station. The corbelling provides a historical bridge back to 1891 when the fire station was itself constructed. It was the contribution of ward councillor Peter Dean, who was also a fireman serving the area for many years.

During the 1980s, SELHAL also began to see its activities in terms that go wider than property management. Service to tenants and providing a contribution to the local community became increasingly important concerns.

Newly appointed staff were becoming deeply involved in the practical issues of housing regeneration such as the layouts and space standards of the terraced houses they were repairing, improving the heating insulation levels and making accommodation accessible to disabled people.

Above: A turn of the century picture of the Werneth Fire Station.
Left: Lady Montgomery, Steve Griffiths and Chairperson Phil Atherton with the remnants of the Werneth fire station in the gardens at Malton street, Coppice.

One example is the donation to the International Year of Shelter for the Homeless in 1987. Staff and tenants organised tea dances at Werneth Park Study Centre which were well attended by many of the company's elderly tenants and staff arranged and ran in a sponsored 10k run. It raised a big cheque!

Collaboration also began to take place with the Social Services department and other voluntary organisations with a view to providing purpose designed accommodation for people with disabilities. Since the early beginnings of designing "accessible" accommodation for older people, SELHAL has developed 200 purpose built units specifically for people with a variety of special needs, including Learning disabilities, people recovering from mental illness, fleeing from domestic violence and stepping stones for young people leaving children's homes.

As this awareness of the needs of the company's customers has grown, so did the willingness of staff to put a little bit back. SELHAL has been making contributions to both local and national housing causes for many years.

By 1990, SELHAL had built 700 homes. The growth in the housing stock and the organisations responsibilities has since grown a pace. By 1998, SELHAL had taken responsibility inside of a company group structure for a smaller Housing Association, the Community Relations Housing Association. The Group now owns 1400 homes and manages another 400 homes at Primrose Bank. The Management Contract is an example of one of the many imaginative housing products that SELHAL has been offering in recent years. Oldham Council, in looking for innovative solutions to increasing housing investment in its own council homes, selected SELHAL to manage and refurbish 400 flats and houses. It is a complex estate that is characterised by a complicated mixture of housing layout and construction type. £5.2 million has been spent since 1993. The project has proved a widely regarded success with high satisfaction levels reported by the people of Primrose Bank.

SELHAL is now a mature housing business that is building or rehabilitating a steady stream of new homes, providing high quality housing management services for both its own tenants and that of others, is an innovator in the area of community care and supported housing and is always looking at ways to add value to the community that is Oldham.

Above and top: Two examples of quality housing offered by the association.
Left: *The cheque for the amount raised for International Year of Shelter for the Homeless.*

The Roxy Cinema - entertainment with a touch of nostalgia

The ground on which the Roxy was built was once occupied by two rows of cottages. One was Canal Street where the famous Failsworth writer, Ben Brierley, once lived and Henfield Row. The latter is possibly better remembered as Muffin Row, referred to by Brierley in some of his writings. The cinema stands at the junction of Hollins Road and Manchester Road and was built in 1937 by Percy Hamer, uncle of the present manager, Kenneth Blair.

It was not an innovation. In the thirties there was an abundance in Oldham, as in most towns, of theatres and cinemas. They offered happy hours of escape for operatives who slaved daily in the dust and grime of the factories and cotton mills which were Oldham's heritage. It is sad that the Roxy is the only surviving local example of the entertainment emporia which gave so much enjoyment to the parents and grand-parents of the present citizens of Oldham.

The doors were opened to the public on Monday, December 20th 1937 to a gala showing of 'Fire over England' with a special souvenir programme put out on each seat.

The first manager to be appointed was Mr Basil Boddington. Born in South Africa, he could list big game hunting, coffee plantation management and gold prospecting among his former occupations.

Above: An early advertising feature from the 1940s.

This picture: The Roxy in 1937, before the Cinema opened to the public. The Roxy cost about £23,000 to build, a staggering amount at the time.

> ## "ONE OF 28 CINEMAS IN THE NORTH WEST, THE ROXY HELD 1,600 PATRONS AND COST £23,000 TO BUILD."

He had also been a commercial traveller, an artist, an engine-greaser and a boxing-booth showman. Unfortunately, after a ten-year period of successful management, Mr Boddington committed some offence that caused him to be dismissed in disgrace by the directors of the cinema company. Kenneth Blair senior took over as manager. He allowed his son to work as an apprentice in the projection room. Starting in 1959, Kenneth junior progressed into the management side of the cinema and became the next manager when his father died in 1977.

Under the present board of directors, on which are representatives of the original shareholders, The Roxy has met the challenge of other entertainment media and not succumbed, like other former independent Oldham cinemas, or the town centre cinemas of the national circuits, which failed to provide the people of Oldham with filmed entertainment when cinemas became economically unviable. Inside The Roxy there are still some traces of the theatre many older patrons remember but the cinema is virtually unrecognisable from that which opened 60 years ago.

Above right: Phyliss Jones, an early Roxy usherette. A formidable lady in any cinema, the usherette was responsible for maintaining quiet in the hall, often at the expense of excited youngsters who found that keeping quiet was almost impossible. Many children were hauled out into the street after numerous warnings, only to regret their actions when their friends were able to stay inside to watch the film.
Right: Five cinemas can be seen in this map of Oldham, showing the competition The Roxy had to suffer.

The current managing directors, Ken Blair and Mike Morris have developed the business on a scale where it now competes equally with the national multiplex opera-tions, boasting seven screens equipped with the latest technology, a large licenced bar, three large sales kiosks serving everything from chocolates to hot dogs and pizzas, and a pick and mix sweet selection area.

The new M66 motorway link will bring many more people to The Roxy's doors where they will enjoy their experience in a truly unique cinema.

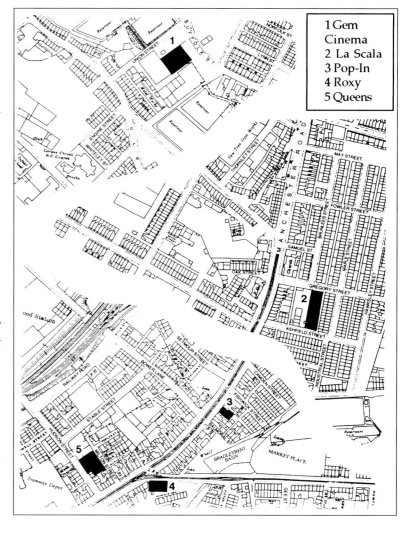

1 Gem Cinema
2 La Scala
3 Pop-In
4 Roxy
5 Queens

The Oldham College - the Platt family legacy to the town

The establishment now known as The Oldham College was given to the people of Oldham on January 1st 1893 by the Platt family, of the famous Platt Brothers textile dynasty.

Before this time the building had housed the former School of Science and Art. The building (on Union Street) was later sold to Oldham Corporation for the sum of £8,750 when the school transferred to new premises in Ashcroft Street in 1897. This building, known then as the Municipal Technical College had to be extended in 1927 to house the rapidly expanding school.

Demand for knowledge grew as the twentieth century went on and the need for technical knowledge became ever more necessary as the Second World War became a serious threat. At that time and during the war the school expanded to

The building of the new college began on Rochdale Road in 1950 and was completed in 1954. The opening ceremony on 5th October was a grand occasion, attended by all the local dignitaries and many townsfolk, with the Viscount Woolton of Liverpool giving the speech.

The Ashcroft Road premises were kept on as an annex for the science department until September 1966 when it also transferred to the Rochdale Road site.

such an extent that it had to use six buildings during the day and twelve in the evenings to accommodate the growing number of students and associated courses.

By the end of World War II, however, the Ashcroft Street premises could no longer offer the space required and new premises became urgently required.

In 1947 the Corporation took the decision to erect a new College of Further Education. Oldham visionaries proposed a new combined Municipal College of Commerce, a School of Arts & Crafts and a Women's Institute. This combined venture would cost £900,000.

The proposals were approved a year later by the Ministry of Education with one proviso; that only the college that would teach the major technologies would be built. It was a blow but the corporation agreed.

Now part of Oldham's heritage, the college offers full and part time courses for people of all ages. The courses have adapted to modern needs as have the people who use the college. Technology and times have changed since the early days and The Oldham College is proud to be able to accommodate these drastic changes.

Above: The Ashcroft Street premises pictured here at the turn of the century.
Facing page, top right: A charming picture taken in the 1930s of an Oldham family playing in the street.
Left: This picture, believed to be from the 1950s shows students experimenting with telephone equipment.
Top: Another 1950s scene, thought to be in the Ashcroft Road Science laboratory, illustrates the kind of technical equipment in use at that time.

Siemens - meeting demand countrywide

Siemens Measurements Limited is the UK market leader in the development and manufacture of electronic electricity and gas meters for domestic and commercial industrial applications. Based in Oldham, the 13-acre factory site is one of the most modern assembly plants of its type in Europe, employing more than 450 people.

The Company was formed in 1978 as a joint venture between Ferranti's metering department and Siemens metering interests in the UK. Siemens, despite being a German company has had a presence in England for over 130 years.

The purpose of the joint venture was to develop a new range of meters using advanced technology and state of the art production systems capable of making improved meters at lower cost.

In October 1985 Siemens plc acquired 100% equity in the company. An interim name, FML, was then used until the company was renamed Siemens Measurements Limited in January 1991.

Following the involvement of Siemens, the site went through several stages of demolition, rebuilding and refitting with the latest technology manufacturing equipment.

In April 1989, HRH Duke of Kent was invited to open the new factory and many officials and dignitaries visited the site, including Sir Cyril Smith MP.

In 1988 Siemens Measurements Limited launched a new family of totally electronic electricity meters. These formed the basis of the business for the next eight years. Variations on the basic theme included single phase meters both for prepayment systems and for complex tariffs, using the national radio-teleswitching service, and polyphase meters for commercial and industrial use.

At the end of a six year development program the company launched the world's first electronic domestic gas meter in 1994. This was successfully sold to British Gas in an initial £20 million contract and is now the leading electronic meter purchased by Transco. This new meter design uses ultrasonic measuring techniques to provide a more accurate and stable meter than the existing mechanical designs.

The latest development from Siemens is the range of Adaptive electricity and gas meters. These have been created to meet the needs of the deregulated energy market as we move into the next millennium. Being modular in construction they will enable energy suppliers to simply add modules to the basic meter to provide new functions and services for their customers.

Above: Ferranti invented this electricity meter in London. This advertisement dates from 1884.
Left: The main assembly line in the meter department at the Hollinwood factory c 1953/54.
Below: Hollinwood - the traditional headquarters of the Ferranti Group. This picture dates from the early 1950s.

FERRANTI
PATENT
ELECTRICITY METER.

HOUSE & SHIP FORM
INVENTOR AND MANUFACTURER
S. ZIANI DE FERRANTI
Office, ST BENET CHAMBERS, Fenchurch Street
Works, 57TH HATTON GARDEN, E.C. LONDON.

JW Lees - independent family brewers since 1828

There's a proud tradition behind J.W. Lees, going back to 1828 when John Lees, a cotton manufacturer, sold his business. He intended to retire but found leisure not to his liking. He therefore bought a row of cottages, together with some land in Middleton Junction and went into business as a brewer of porter and ale. In fact it was not until 1839 that Middleton Junction took its name from the station sited there, on George Stephenson's Littleborough to Manchester railway line.

In 1876 the Brewery had become so successful that a new brewhouse needed to be built. John Willie Lees, the founder's grandson, set to this task with relish and completed what was then considered to be one of the most modern brewhouses in the country opposite the original brewhouse on the same site. J.W. Lees still brews there today and even uses some of the original fermenting vessels from 1876, although there has been considerable modernisation, extensions and improvements to the brewery.

Modernisation at J.W. Lees has always been carefully carried out and the environment is still dominated by wood, copper and classic 19th century tower architecture. In the cross beamed brewhouse and the cellars beneath the yard visitors to the brewery can see beer at every stage of production.

Incidentally, the Boardroom at J.W. Lees is recognisable to millions of ITV viewers as the headquarters of Newton & Ridley, brewers to Coronation Street's Rover's Return.

J.W. Lees never forgot the traditional methods of brewing and conditioning real beer, so they were well placed to take advantage of recent renewed interest in real ales. Just as it was over 170 years ago, the beers at J.W. Lees are still brewed in the time-honoured way of starting with only the very best malted barley, hops and yeast. Many national and international awards have been won by J.W. Lees for their superb beers and lagers.

Most recently Moonraker Strong Ale has been voted Gold Medal Winner in the

Above: *A picture of Greengate Brewery in 1876. This is still the company's headquarters today.*
Top left: *John Lees, founder of the brewery.*
Left: *Greengate Brewery in 1828.*

Barley Wines Category in the CAMRA Champion Winter Beer of Britain award in 1997/1998.

J.W. Lees's Vintage Harvest Ale, referred to as the 'King of Beers' by internationally renowned Beer writer Michael Jackson, is a world classic. It dates back to 1986 when after a good dinner there was a conversation bemoaning the invasion of overseas brewers into British markets. So Head Brewer Giles Dennis, aided and abetted by Chairman Richard Lees-Jones set about creating the Best of British.

The result was J.W. Lees Vintage Harvest Ale, a special beer, brewed only once a year from the first of the season's hops and malt. It's one of the strongest beers in the world at 11.5% ABV and is fermented for a very long time in traditional 'rounds' before being bottled for release in the first week in December every year. The irony of the tale is that the last remaining stocks of past vintages has just been exported to America where beer enthusiasts can't get enough of Vintage Harvest Ale!

J.W. Lees values its special relationship with CAMRA, the Campaign for Real Ale, and is keen to build on cask beer sales when others are opting to brew modern 'mixed gas' smooth beers which are easier to dispense and look after. To this end J.W. Lees's beers are always available at CAMRA beer festivals up and down the country. Moonraker Strong Ale is a favourite and at 7.5% ABV is one of the strongest beers available throughout the year in the UK.

J.W. Lees is very much a family business. Not only have six generations of the founder's family worked in the Brewery but there are many generations of local people who have either worked in the Brewery or held licenses running one or more of the Brewery's 170 pubs.

J.W. Lees is very much part of the local community with strong links with many areas, most famously with Oldham Athletic Association Football Club.

Top: *A dray from the 1970s, on this occasion being used in a carnival.*
Above: *J. W. Lees Cask Bitter.*
Left: *The modern day Greengate Brewery. Little has changed from the outside since 1828.*

Frank Warren Ltd - Three generations of company commitment

Frank Warren began his own business in 1950. As a Plumbers Merchant, Frank and his son Seth started the business on Terrace Street in a row of terraced houses that incorporated a laundry machine manufacturer.

Having removed all the old laundry machines the resulting space was shelved out using old lard boxes acquired from Park Cake Bakery in Oldham.

Although successful as a plumbers merchant it soon became apparent that the business could expand by stocking Engineering and Electrical supplies and today the company is better known for this type of equipment.

The firm remained at these first premises for 25 years. In 1974 after the death of his father, Seth

Above: Seth Warren with his delivery van. This picture was taken in the mid 1950s.
Below: The shop in Terrace Street in 1951. The houses that can be seen in this picture were gradually taken over by the firm and eventually demolished to make way for new premises.

expansion of the power tool department.

Stock now covers an area in excess of 20,000 square feet and with three delivery vehicles, stock is distributed throughout Greater Manchester. The business is open six days a week and offers a personal service to all its customers. This includes free delivery and advice on product selection. The company prides itself on being able to source almost any product required. A tribute to the number of years in business.

then reorganised the business and moved into newer and much larger premises at the rear. The old terrace houses were demolished. At this time the business was also made a limited company.

Over the next 15 years the company increased its stock and turnover to become a major wholesaler in the Oldham area. Seth introduced yet another line of supply by opening a Power Tool department for both sales and repair.

Having returned from 10 years in the USA as a data base analyst Seth's son Mark started as joint managing director of the company in 1992.

Mark now runs the business after his father's retirement in 1993. Under Mark's direction a new office block has been built and a fresh image has been adopted for the company. Free space vacated by the old offices has now been reclaimed for the

All major brand names in Engineering and Electrical supplies are to be found at Frank Warren Ltd, again a result of many years of business and a close co-operation with suppliers.

Oldham is a strong base for any company and expansion is clearly on the horizon for this one.

Above: Mark Warren, third generation of the family.
Top: The premises as seen in 1975, now demolished.
Below: The new premises of Frank Warren Ltd. The rebuilding of the office block took about six months.

Oldham work displayed in the Tate Gallery

The Oldham foam and fibre specialists, Platt and Hill are proud of the knowledge that, behind every Turner sketch and painting in the Tate's Clore Gallery extension there is a Platt and Hill fire-retardant wall filling, helping to protect this important part of the nation's heritage.

When the firm began life in 1889 it had a rather less glamorous role. The founders were John James Platt, a textile engineer from Delph and John Hill, a Prudential manager from the Oldham office. They took premises at Beehive Mill, Lamb Street, off Medlock Street and began by processing cotton flock for furniture makers, exploiting the demand for horsehair suites which were then all the rage in Victorian drawing rooms. They used cleaning, garnetting, carding, cross laying and mill puff equipment with cotton waste from the cotton mills. Cotton felt was later manufactured for the bedding, furniture and wadded quilt trade.

To describe Platt and Hill as a family firm would be misleading. It is a two-family firm and its members are still 'Oldhamers', unlike so many mill owners who made their money and then moved away to live in Wales or the Home Counties.

John James Platt worked for another textile firm, J & T Wilde, before setting up in business with John Hill from Leicestershire. For the first 70 years of its life the firm operated from the now-demolished Beehive Mill at Mumps.

John Platt's grandson, Clarence joined the firm in 1923 when it employed less than twenty people and was ticking along rather than making a lot of money. He 'did a bit of

everything', learning the trade as he went along. In those days groups of men would come along looking for casual work. They would work for a few hours until they had enough money for a pint or two and would be paid up by lunchtime.

By the time Clarence's son, Philip took over there was a permanent work force in the region of over

Above: John James Platt and John Hill, founders of the company.
Right: The fleet from the 1940s.

"IN 1969 DUNLOPILLO TOOK A MINORITY SHAREHOLDING IN THE COMPANY WHICH GAVE THE OLDHAM COMPANY GOOD ACCESS TO HIGH QUALITY FOAM AND EXTRA MANAGEMENT EXPERTISE."

two hundred. John Hill's great grandsons, David and Anthony were Philip Platt's co-directors. The two families tended to operate in different areas of the business, the Platts on the production side and the Hills on sales. Philip Platt and Anthony and David Hill rotated the job of company chairman, a novel arrangement but one which suited all parties and promoted good relations.

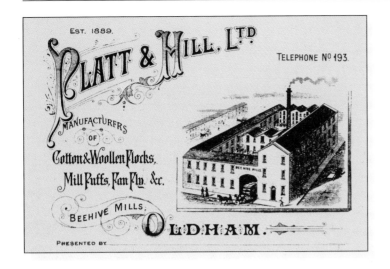

In 1969 Dunlopillo took a minority shareholding in the company which gave the Oldham company good access to high quality foam and extra management expertise. Platt & Hill have licence agreements with Dunlopillo to use their well known household name on a wide variety of products that are manufactured for retail customers. The largest product range for this joint venture is the pillow market. Many well known high street retailers display Dunlopillo brand pillows manufactured by Platt & Hill Ltd.

A key factor in the firm's commercial success has been the development and use of top quality foam and fibre fillings, specially treated to prevent fire-spread. This is important in household furnishings where poisonous fumes are often the main cause of fire deaths. When the government introduced new safety standards in March 1989, Platt and Hill were well ahead of most of the competition in this respect, in some cases teaching other firms how to do things. This left the UK industry and Platt and Hill in particular in a strong position to push into Europe in the early nineties.

In the period since the second war many coarse-spinning firms have disappeared, not having the ability and resources to adapt in an ever-changing market. Platt and Hill's survival owes a lot to its move into specialist fillings. They not only survived but expanded from the Mumps site to the Wellington Mills at Greenfield, then, in 1976,

to a large factory at Belgrave Mills. The company purchased a second factory on the Belgrave Mills site in 1994 (see photograph below), carrying out an extensive renovation and modernisation programme on the old cotton mill. The four year rolling schedule of work will not be completed until well into 1998.

Currently the company supplies industries in upholstery, bedding, apparel and leisure furniture. Their main customers are G Plan, Marks & Spencer, Argos and the John Lewis Partnership. It uses petro-chemical based products, synthetic fibres and foam. Natural products used are feathers and cotton. Their ISO 9002 registration attests to their quality. They are often more expensive than their competitors but are awarded business because of their consistent quality standards.

Over 100 years ago, it was a member of the Platt family who went off to register the company, hence the name Platt & Hill Ltd. The Hills have always maintained that the company should have been registered with the names in alphabetical order (ie Hill & Platt). A fifth generation of Hills and Platts are now involved in the business. In middle management positions; John Platt, Nicholas Hill and Andrew Hill, all in their mid twenties will soon be in a position to guide the company beyond the millennium, into a second hundred years of trading.

Above: A business card dating from the turn of the century.
Below: The modern premises in Belgrave Mill.

JH Humphreys - more than a century of engineering in Oldham

JH Humphreys & Sons began as a family concern, in premises close to the Colliseum, in 1891. Later it became part of Edgar Allen, a Sheffield based engineering group. Then, just over ten years ago, it returned to local family ownership.

For more than a century the company has been a market leader in magnetic chucks and their products are known in engineering circles the world over. Their customers include Land Rover, GKN Metals and British Steel Corporation.

Very few people outside the engineering industry will know what an electro-magnetic chuck is but most people will be very familiar with the ordinary household products and motor car components that are made by using them. They are pieces of engineering hardware that hold a component in place without brackets, whilst a grinder or miller machines it. J H Humphreys & Sons, based in Werneth, is probably the only British manufacturer of these often large devices.

Whilst the manufacture of electro-magnetic chucks is the core business of Humphreys, the company, in recent years, has widened its range of products to include Shear Blades and Wear Plates which are components of the scrap paper and general refuse reclamation industry. Humphreys have also developed into the blade industry, particularly granulator blades for plastics and rubber reclamation. Business in the last named product is growing rapidly.

The company employs thirty people in its Milne Street, Werneth factory and many of them have spent much of their working lives with the company, long service awards being nothing out of the ordinary.

Despite the company's adherence to tradition, it is forward looking in its use of modern technology in production methods. Above all the company is proud of its Oldham roots and is pleased to carry the name of the town into engineering concerns throughout the country.

Above: An electro magnet which is holding a magnetic chuck. The picture dates from 1974.
Above left: Some of the staff in the 1960s.
Left: A late 1940s view of Humphrey's Werneth factory. All production takes place here, from raw steel blanks to the finished product.

Salomon Frankenhuis - the man whose vision had far-reaching potential

Frankenhuis is a business with a long and successful history. It was established in 1884 by Salomon Frankenhuis who envisaged the business potential of recycling textile raw materials by processing them through machinery such as a willowing plant. He laid the foundations for the company in Haaksbergen, Holland at a time when the cotton industry was burgeoning in Holland and in the neighbouring German border region.

Ten years later, in 1894, his son, Heiman, came into what was by then a flourishing business and the present day name, S. Frankenhuis en Zoon BV was established. Since that time, five generations of the family have been at the helm of the company.

Above: The Anchor Mill blackout during World War II. Above left: Salomon Frankenhuis, founder of the company. Below: A state visit by Prince Bernhardt of the Netherlands in the Second World War brought him to Anchor Mill where he was met by the workers who were sorting out raw cotton.

Being a family business they all worked along similar lines - the buying and selling of raw materials, maintenance of the machinery and running the plant were a joint effort.

There followed four decades of continuous growth and prosperity during which time Heiman Frankenhuis' son, Salomon, joined the company. His subsequent involvement with the Frankenhuis enterprise revealed a brilliant

business acumen which led the company into a truly international field extending the operation to the four corners of the world.

Above: Sorting burnt cotton during the Second World War.
Right (both pictures): In 1955 Eric Webb was a warehouse assistant with the company. In the main picture, taken in 1955 he was fifteen years old (on the left). Today he is managing director (small picture) after voicing his ambition at his interview for the job of warehouse assistant.

under the name of King & Darbyshire Ltd. finally changing its name to S. Frankenhuis & Son Limited on 14th April, 1959.

The Haaksbergen plant remains on the same site today, although the English Company moved from its Anchor Mill site in 1995 to purpose built premises at Broadgate, Oldham. The company has specialised in supplying healthcare, spinning, felting and bedding industries with raw materials ending up as surgical dressings, nonwovens, yarns, fibre fillings, upholstery felts and quilts amongst many others.

In 1935, fearful of the developments in Germany the company was established in England.

The company appointed Jac de Haas as their England agent and in 1937 he bought Anchor Mill for £3,000. The company was incorporated in 1939

Above: A baling press powered by a water pump.
Below: Bales of burnt cotton can be seen in this World War II picture, waiting to be re-sorted for spinning.

United Kingdom, Frankenhuis supplies its products to all the major users of cotton waste and man-made fibres.

After many years during which it was run by descendants of the Frankenhuis family, the company was sold in 1995 to Chris Crowley, owner of U.S. firm Cherokee Textiles, Inc. He appointed the present Managing Director, Eric Webb, who as a 15 year old boy had stood in Jac de Haas' office and told him that his ambition was to one day be sitting in that chair - and today he is.

As very little of the company's material comes from within the

The company has a well stocked warehouse so that it can supply its customers at short notice.

The company purchases cotton, cotton waste and man-made fibres from countries all over the world. Sources include China, Pakistan, USA, Brazil and Finland and virtually anywhere else in the world where the fibre is produced. A market leader in the

United Kingdom it has to be expert at sourcing exactly what the customer needs, at the right prices. This commitment to efficiency and quality is what has led the company onwards over the years and it is this which will lead it into the 21st century.

Top: Anchor Mill as seen in February 1989. Frankenhuis used these premises until 1995 when it moved to Broadgate, Oldham, into purpose built premises (above).
Left: Chris Crowley, President of the American Company, Cherokee Textiles Inc., is also sole owner of Frankenhuis.

Generations of Oldham craftsmanship

There is always a romantic appeal about a long lived firm, as Emanuel Whittaker Ltd of Oldham, founded in 1837 can certainly claim to be. In the intervening 160 years this business has played a notable part in the commercial history of the town.

The Whittaker family traces its history in Oldham back to 1690. There has always been a builder in the family, but it was 22 year old Emanuel Whittaker who founded his own business which grew into one of Oldham's most respected companies.

A history of the family was compiled in 1847 by a William Whittaker. He refers to a relative, George, as "one of the principle masters in Oldham". The description seems well founded since the said George built the Oldham Lyceum, pictured below as originally built, before the addition of the Art School. He also built the Greaves Street Gas Works and the Rochdale Road Institution as well as many of the old cotton mills. His business was run from Haggate Lane, now Middleton Road, Royton and he 'lived on the job'.

His business continued to prosper until he died in 1858. He had been the father of eleven daughters and one son, Emanuel, born in 1815. At the age of eleven, Emanuel was put to work bricksetting. After four years of this, he was apprenticed to a joiner. On becoming a master builder in 1845 he set up an independent business at the same address as his father's in Rochdale Road to manufacture joinery and to develop timber merchanting and sawmilling.

At first he used mills in Liverpool to cut the main requirements for sawn timber and carried out some hand sawing on the premises, but in 1849 he took the plunge and became the first person in Oldham to have steam power driven sawing and woodworking machinery. The displacement of the old hand sawers caused some resentment and resulted in an attempt to burn down the mill. Fortunately not a lot of damage was caused, although the culprits were never apprehended.

The business expanded rapidly and in 1853 Emanuel Whittaker got his first contract for the building of a cotton mill. Before long, however, the cotton famine

ruined some rival businesses but Emanuel Whittaker used the time which this recession offered to remodel his premises. His investment was rewarded in the 1870s by a flood of orders for the design and construction of mills.

Emanuel became increasingly absorbed in public affairs, becoming Mayor of Oldham in 1873 and a JP. He died aged 68 in 1882. His elder son, Thomas, managed the business in trust until the coming of age of Emanuel's younger son, Frank in 1889. Frank continued to run the business in his father's name and it became incorporated as a Limited Company in 1908.

A serious fire in 1929 seemed a disaster at the time. Little of the factory remained, the offices were badly damaged but the sheds and timber stock remained largely intact. However, it did enable Frank Whittaker to replan the factory and bring it up to modern standards of layout and machinery.

The following two decades of recession and war saw the company survive with a limited number of employees on maintenance work in mills and

schools and some manufacture for the war effort. Other work during the war was very difficult with so many of the younger men serving in the forces and with timber being strictly rationed.

In 1937 there was a happy gathering at the Central Conservative Club when more than a hundred members of staff were entertained to a dinner and concert in celebration of the company's centenary and the seventieth birthday of Frank Whittaker.

Frank Whittaker died in 1940 and was succeeded by Vernon Whittaker, his nephew and grandson of Emanuel. After the war the company slowly returned to its former self generally, employing about a hundred men in

Above: A letterhead dating from the 1910s.
Top: An early picture of horse drawn transport from about 1850. It was a day's work each week to travel to Manchester Docks to collect timber and a very long pull for the horse up Manchester Road from Hollinwood to Werneth Fire Station with a full load.
Left: The Oldham Lyceum, built by Emanuel Whittaker's father, George, in 1854.

the factory and out on building sites.

In 1972 Vernon died at the age of 71 and his son, Thomas, took over as Chairman, where he remains to the present.

By the 1960s the premises consisted of a variety of buildings and considerable working space. There were five large storage and timber drying sheds with separate areas for hardwoods and softwoods. The machinery was of the latest types and included plant that was new to the north of England. All the machines were electrically driven and the old steam boiler which was originally used to power the factory was retained for the incineration of factory waste to provide sufficient steam for all the heating required in the factory and offices. The premises have since been further modernised and extended to today's 40,000 square feet of floorspace.

The company has always maintained a flexible approach and has readily adapted to new working practices and fashions. It carries out work for clients all over the country on contracts as widely differing from council house refurbishment to the building of a new Job Centre.

Recently the firm manufactured and installed windows for the Mansion House in London and replacement hardwood sliding sash windows for a Listed Building belonging to City University.

One area in which the Company has established a long and well respected reputation is in the design and manufacture of staircases. Made to measure, each staircase is produced to clients' own specifications and in the clients' own choices of timber.

Future plans for the firm include ISO 9000 accreditation and the launching of two speciality lines.

The first being a fully finished and framed door unit complete with furniture made to British Standard requirements for security and fire resistance. The second being a window range, again made to British Standards for security and weather penetration.

However much technology, fashions and building methods change, there will always be a call for the traditional, time served craftsman that only comes from long experience and deep understanding of the trade.

To this end, the company maintains its long standing policy of training apprentices in all facets of the business irrespective of the fluctuations of trade. Emanuel Whittaker Ltd can offer its customers the highest standards of skill and service.

Facing page, top: A view of the joiners' shop in 1938. It is quite poignant to realise that some of the younger men pictured here would soon be called up to fight in the Second World War. Indeed, it would have been foremost on all their minds.
Facing page, bottom: A view of the sawmill in 1938.
***Below:** The company's centenary dinner which took place in the Oldham Central Conservative Club in 1937.*

Success against all odds

The company of George Hill (Oldham) Limited, timber merchants and moulding manufacturers was established by George Hill on 11th November 1919, exactly one year to the hour after armistice day.

Together with his son, Wilfred, George set up premises in Water Street in converted cottages previously used for fish curing. The site is now occupied by Oldham Police Station. Three years later, George Frank Hill, George's younger son, joined the business, on leaving school at age 14.

In the beginning George and his sons shared the work between them equally, the warehousing, moulding and selling was done by whoever was available at the time. It wasn't until the 1950s when the two sons specialised - Wilfred controlled purchasing and Frank looked after production.

The business continued to grow, in spite of the depression of the 1930s and further premises were acquired at Lady Street, Oldham (the former Oldham Ice Company) and later the company bought land on Lord Street, adjacent to the Lady Street facility.

George Hill died in 1947 and the control of the business passed to his two sons. Both sons worked for over fifty years before retiring.

By the late 1950s the company had expanded their less than ideal three town centre premises, all of which were lost when the Council took over ownership of them for redevelopment (The Police Station and St Mary's Estate).

As a result of this, in 1960 an old mill site of five acres was purchased from the council and operations were transferred to there. The site, Scottfield Sawmills, was ideal for the company's needs, despite early problems with old mill lodges, slopes and the odd ash pit. All these problems were ironed out along the way and the company has made this site its home ever since. A further adjacent five acres was purchased in 1980.

The company has grown over the years, opening a Sale Branch at Glebelands Road, Sale in 1975 and a Bolton branch in 1983.

These moves proved an instant success. One of the qualities that has led to this accomplishment is the dedication to quality. Timber is sought from all over the world and only the very best is used.

It is also the little touches that make the difference between success and failure. Hill's believe that all items on their stock list should be in stock so that the customer is not kept waiting. They also offer a free collection and delivery service.

Highly skilled moulders can produce special period mouldings from both softwood and hardwood. Thus, it can produce mouldings suitable for listed buildings. Also, keeping in with the modern trend, it has a 'drive-thru' builders merchants.

Still owned by the Hill family, three generations on, the firm intends to expand its customer base, as well as building on the current premises to excel service in the locality.

The firm has had a long and diverse past, but has kept its personal touch throughout any hardships which have occurred along the way. It is a characteristic which has led to success and Hill's know that it is this attribute, along with the promise of good value and quality service that will lead it into the 21st century.

Above: A special version of 'It's a Knockout' was held by the company in December 1977 to announce the opening of a new panel cutting department. It was hosted by TV's Stuart Hall (inset).

Below: The company's 50th anniversary took place in 1969. Here the proud family pose for a celebratory photograph.

Facing page, top right: George Hill, pictured with his wife on a trip to the seaside in the mid 1940s. George's business survived, despite the depression of the 1930s and when he died in 1947, he left his family a thriving company which still proudly bears his name today.

Facing page, bottom: An early family photograph of George and his family. His two sons entered the business with him at early ages.

Tommy Gartside - the man with 'Mill building fever'

More than a hundred years ago, Mr T E Gartside, more familiarly known as Tommy, took the first step that would lead to three generations of his family being closely connected with the cotton textile industry. The step was to apply for and obtain the post of junior clerk at Royton Spinning Company. He had obviously found his metier, since he rose to become Managing Director and then Chairman of Shiloh Spinning Company Ltd, a position currently held by his grandson, Mr Edmund Gartside.

The Shiloh Spinning Company

On February 17th 1874, eleven Royton men, none of them wealthy, decided to pool their resources to float a cotton-spinning company. Royton already had the first cotton mill in Lancashire which had been built at Thorp Clough in 1764, so the industry had been established in the area for some time. The Shiloh Spinning Company was named after an old wooden mill, partially burned down, that remained on the chosen site. It was a name with good, honest biblical associations, which did the new company no harm, but the original source of the name was most likely the US cotton town which had recently been supplying Lancashire with raw cotton.

On March 14th 1874, applications for shares in the new company were invited. A good many of these were taken up by mill workers who risked their life savings. Mill finance, as the custom was then, consisted of loan accounts to cover the cost of building and equipment. Loans were guaranteed by nothing more than the character and reputation of the promoters, but both they and the bankers were local folk who knew all about each other.

The company became formally incorporated under its first chairman, Henry Lowe. Asa Lees of Oldham obtained the contract for supplying machinery. Cannily, the Shiloh Spinning Company insisted on the old engine from the half-burnt-down wooden mill being traded in as part of the deal. In 1893, the company invested in modern communications technology by acquiring a telephone.

In the following year Tommy Gartside began his career with Shiloh. It lasted from 1894 to 1941. By the turn of the century he was on the board of four separate companies all later to become part of the group. He was a prime mover in the flotation of Vine, Park and Grape mills and a director from their incorporation.

There was further expansion of the cotton industry in the years leading up to the First World War and four more mills were built in the

Above: Col JB Gartside DSO, MC, TD, DL, JP, who succeeded as Chairman in 1941. *Top:* T.E. (Tommy) Gartside J.P., founder of the company which is still under his family's direction today. *Left:* Captain, the horse which served the Royton Spinning Company from 1884 until 1905.

1909 but by 1911 Mr Gartside was getting another bout of 'mill-building fever'. He decided to build another mill. Again, Asa Lees agreed to supply equipment on Mr Gartside's terms when they were promised the contracts for two mills instead of one. Thus the Park (No 2 Mill) and the Park & Sandy (No 2 Mill) were built together in 1912/13 off the same plans, and there was a race to spin the first cop of yarn.

From 1884 to 1905 the mills were faithfully served by Captain, a horse that trans-

Gartside Group. Mr Gartside had previously bought Highfield Mill in Bleasdale Street and a new company was formed, Park Mill (Royton) Ltd, to run it. The mill was renamed Park. Other companies too were building cotton mills and extending production and trade.

Shiloh itself was making steady progress under Mr Gartside's management. In 1905 extensions were built to No 2 mill and in 1907 Mr Gartside became chairman of the company. There was a recession in

ported cotton and yarn from Royton railway station to the mills and from there to customers. He was housed in special stables adjacent to the mill. Every May Day in that period the carters were each provided with a new suit and bowler hat. The horses, bedecked and splendid, were paraded past each of the directors' houses.

Above: Park Mill, built in 1912.
Below: Gala day in the early 1950s, a day when the families of employees could become involved.

The 1914-1918 War

Mr Gartside's son, John, then production manager, was one of the first to join up. He became a pilot in the Royal Flying Corps and later was seriously injured.

The war benefited the cotton industry as extra production was required to clothe the troops. There were serious labour problems though.

A dreadful accident occurred in December 1914 when the huge flywheel of No 2 mill burst. The engine house was completely shattered and huge lumps of cast steel were hurled into the air. Fortunately no-one was in the engine house at the time, but a cardroom jobber was killed and a tenter was seriously injured. Mr Gartside was away in Liverpool buying cotton. Major repairs were needed and 350 workers were unemployed until they were completed.

In 1916 Gartside became chairman of Holly, Vine and Grape. He played his part in the local community, being a JP and a councillor.

Above: The visit of Prime Minister, Harold Macmillan to Roy in 1959, just after his election to office.
Right: Shiloh trainees being taught how to identify faults in yarn. The picture dates from the very early 70s.

Post-War

After the war there was still a demand for Lancashire cotton. In 1919 voluntary restrictions were no longer asked for and there was prosperity in the industry until the twenties. Like many of the mills around them, Gartside mills recapitalised, but responsibly, not in the reckless fashion of some others. After reconstruction the company was renamed Shiloh Mills Ltd. Outstanding loans were paid off completely and the whole of the original share capital was redeemed. Holly, Vine and Park restructured in the same way.

In 1919 Roy Mill was added to the Gartside empire.

The difficult twenties

Short time in all the mills led at times to industrial disputes and strikes. In 1925 the directors of Grape Mill carried out capital reconstruction as the other mills had done.

When Gartside decided, in these economic conditions, to build another, larger, mill, the newspapers referred to it as 'Tommy's Folly'. He ignored his critics and went ahead, naming his new mill 'The Elk'. This time its machinery was provided by Platts of Oldham.

The Elk was the last mule spinning mill to be built in Lancashire and to be financed in the old way by loan accounts. In spite of everyone's misgivings it was very successful and still stands today in a commanding position close to the M62.

In 1927 a great storm flooded Royton. Parts of both the company's mills were flooded and a wall in No 1 mill collapsed. This disaster proved so expensive that shareholders' dividends were reduced.

The 1940s and 1950s

In 1941, on the death of Mr T E (Tommy) Gartside, Mr J B Gartside became chairman of Shiloh.

In 1946 the mills were reopened after the Second World War and were glad of government grants for new machinery in 1948.

To qualify for these grants, the mills had to be re-organised into larger companies. Mr JB Gartside first formed the Royton Textile Corporation in 1949, a merger of four of the family spinning companies, and then four years later he grouped the remaining mills into the larger company, Shiloh Spinners Ltd. He was Chairman of both these groups until his retirement. With electrification in 1957, the engine in No 2 mill was stopped. 1959 brought a visit from prime minister Harold Macmillan to Roy mill. Soon afterwards Shiloh No 2, Park and Vine were closed under the Government re-organisation scheme. Mr J B Gartside retired and was later succeeded by Mr Edmund Gartside as Managing Director of Shiloh.

In 1968, there was another accident, which ultimately created legal history. The No. 2 mill tower dropped during the course of demolition on to the head office block, causing extensive damage. The company brought an action against the demolition company which, several years later, was finally resolved in Shiloh's favour by a judgement in the House of Lords.

Towards the end of the century

The history of Shiloh differs from that of many similar firms in that, both at the end of the 19th century and in the middle of the 20th it survived crises by anticipation. It saw new trends coming and was not afraid to diversify. Thus it became the UK's first cotton spinner to be awarded BS 5750 certification.

In 1996 Shiloh lived up to its tradition of 'bucking the trend' by purchasing the last remaining spinning mills of Courtaulds Textiles. Consequently the Swan Lane Mill in Bolton and the locally based Chadderton Mill joined the group on 1st January 1997. This made Shiloh not only the biggest cotton spinner in the UK, but the only remaining spinner of any significance. Shiloh now has four spinning units supplying yarns for a wide range of fabrics from knitwear and high quality furnishing fabrics to conveyor belts, bath mats and mops. They are proud of the British Standards 'Kite' mark on their goods. The firm's traditional mainstay, spinning, is buoyant in spite of problems in the industry.

The firm has further diversified into the retail market in health care, geared towards an ageing population. It specialises too in the rapid application of non-woven materials for industrial protection, products made increasingly necessary by the huge range of hazardous materials in industry.

Edmund Gartside still thinks there is a good future in spinning. Though the future in conventional yarns is bleak the company continues to prosper by producing speciality yarns and by giving a first class service and quick response to customer requirements that foreign competition cannot give.

Above: David Trippier MP (right) presents the BSI certificate to director Darrell Shaw at Park Mill in 1990.
Right: Managing director Edmund Gartside, grandson of the famous TE Gartside, whose family still hold 25 per cent of the plc's shares.

Changing with the times

In 1875 a textile engineer, Benjamin Lees founded a business to manufacture looms in Ashley Street, Westwood, Oldham. Since then, six generations of his family have served the company on the same site where the premises have progressively expanded.

Soon, the workers at Ashley Mill were principally weavers, using Lancashire spun cotton on belt driven looms to produce bandage and flannelette goods. A specialist weaving shed still remains, weaving lints and tubular wovens and high quality raising cloths for niche markets, but the business now focuses, as the company's van signs indicate, on added value, processing principally impregnation and coating.

Mr P.B. Lees, the current Chairman and Managing Director, explained, "Like many other textile manufacturers, Lees-Newsome Ltd has diversified into specialised fabrics and added value processes as the opportunities to trade in conventional materials have declined due to competition from low cost economics, especially within the Third World".

Left: Benjamin Lees, who founded the company in 1875. Six generations of the same family have run the firm since that time.
Below: A picture dating from the 1950s, showing one of the weaving sheds.

raised interlinings, baby products, funeral fabrics and so on. They produce a mixture of traditional based cotton products linked with unique impregnated and coated finishes. Having developed selected products , the company is committed to the maintenance of quality and keeping in close touch with all related technology. They realise that a trained and well qualified staff have potential talents to offer the company and the Management affords them every opportunity to contribute their ideas.

Boots, S.C. Johnson Wax, British Vita, Jeyes and Robinson are included in their customer list.

The company has adapted to new markets and needs as well as taking advantage of opportunities that have been recognised over the years. The First World War, for example was 'Boom-time' for a firm already equipped to manufacture surgical dressings.

In the last eleven years the company has been financially restructured, creating a more compact, cost efficient manufacturing operation, ready to meet new challenges. Currently Lees-Newsome supply companies making or selling cleaning cloths, furniture products, pharmaceutical fabrics,

Above: Dating from 1957, this picture shows the tape sizing process prior to weaving.
Right: Also dating from 1957...baling goods for export.

Over two hundred years of proud history for Wrigley Claydon

When the firm that became Wrigley Claydon was first established over 200 years ago, it was called Henry Barlow. Henry Barlow first worked from a building in Yorkshire Street which later became Forsyths wine and spirit merchants.

Henry served his apprenticeship with a solicitor in Ashton and after being admitted as a solicitor in his own right he settled in Oldham where he soon set up his own practice, later taking on a partner, a Mr James Whitehead.

On Henry's death, his eldest son, William became a partner and the firm became known as Messrs. Whitehead & Barlow.

By the late 1850s the firm had become known as Radcliffe & Murray. Henry Wrigley joined in 1859 and when George Spack Claydon joined him in 1885 the name Wrigley & Claydon was adopted.

This name survived many changes and successions of partners who practiced with the firm until the 1970s when it joined forces with the practice of Armstrong Whittaker and Ogden (formerly Armstrong Taylor and Whittaker).

Above: Henry Barlow, founder of the oldest firm of solicitors in Oldham.
Right: The chronology of the firm dating from before 1798 until the present day.

Once amalgamated it became known as Wrigley Claydon & Armstrongs. The new partnership was formed on January 1st 1972.

The origins of Armstrong Taylor & Whittaker's practice can be traced back to the 1870s when John Armstrong set up office in Clegg Street, moving to the then newly built Williams Deacon Bank Chambers on Church Terrace in 1939.

John Armstrong was the last part-time Clerk of the Peace for the Oldham Borough Quarter Sessions, just as his Junior partner, Frank Whittaker was the last part-time Clerk to the Justices, retiring in 1963. Henry Barlow had for many years been Clerk to the Magistrates and may have been the first Clerk to the Justices in Oldham and this tradition of active participation in the legal life of the town has been a

Henry Barlow
Commenced practice in Yorkshire Street before 1798
|
Barlow & Whitehead
formed when Henry Barlow took on a partner, Mr Whitehead
|
Whitehead and Barlow
Formed after Henry's death with the partnership change to his son, William
|
Barlow & Radcliffe
|
Radcliffe & Murray
|
Murray & Wrigley
Formed when Henry Wrigley joined the company in 1859
|
Wrigley & Morecroft
|
Wrigley & Claydon
Formed when Mr George Claydon joined the company in 1885
|
Wrigley Claydon & Tristram
|
Wrigley Claydon & Needham
|
Wrigley Claydon & Fripp
|
Wrigley Claydon, Crozier & Jackson (1937)
|
Wrigley Claydon & Co
|
who in 1972 joined **Armstrong Whittaker & Ogden** to form
|
Wrigley Claydon & Armstrongs
|
Wrigley Claydon
name changed in 1995

feature of the firm and its partners over the two hundred years of its existence.

The Wrigley Claydon practice also worked from Clegg Street in the early 1900s, before moving to a new home in the Prudential Buildings. Only Prudential Buildings could offer the accommodation needed for the enlarged firm at that time but it is expected that a move will be made to the firm's own self contained premises during 1998.

The name Wrigley Claydon & Armstrong was dropped in 1995 as a result of the modern trend to shorten names. It was decided to return to the original name of Wrigley Claydon, which for over a century had been identified as the oldest solicitors practice in Oldham and indeed the oldest continuous business of any sort in the town.

"The tradition of active participation in the legal life of Oldham has been a feature of the firm for its two hundred year existence."

The firm now offers a comprehensive range of facilities for both domestic and personal needs. This includes home buying, accident claims, civil litigation, criminal and family work, company formation and corporate tax planning.

Over two hundred years of continuous practice does not mean that the firm rests on its laurels, expecting work to walk through the door as its right. The firm has had to adapt to modern trends and changes over the years, and with a dedication to modern technology within the office and a commitment to development of personal staff skills, it can look towards the very different world of the 21st century with confidence.

Below: *Left and right at the back - John Colligan and Godfrey Pickles and left to right at the front - David Haines, Wendy Connor, Paul Vincent, Peter Walthall, Vijay Srivastava and John Porter.*

It began with the invasion of Normandy....

The business that became Vitafoam Ltd. and, eventually, British Vita PLC, in part, began in an officers' mess in Witten, Germany, during the British occupation following the end of the Second World War. Two Royal Artillery officers, Norman Grimshaw and Fernley Parker, shared a tent during the invasion of Normandy. They became first friends and then business partners in the 1950s.

Both were married with children and needed employment after demobilisation when army pay would cease. Before the war, Norman Grimshaw had been a laboratory assistant working on latex foam technology for Dunlop in Manchester. He believed that there was an opportunity for the production of latex foam cushioning as the patents relating to the production of latex foam had expired during the war. Fernley Parker had worked as an articled clerk in an accountant's office. He demanded, jocularly, that when Mr. Grimshaw had formed his company and was in a position to employ an accountant, he should take him on. Fernley Parker's textbooks were sent to Germany and the two discussed the principles of book-keeping.

On leaving the army, Norman Grimshaw returned to Dunlop where he met up with a colleague, Graham

Smith. The two later moved to join a firm called Cheshire Latex and with Mr. Grimshaw's and Mr. Smith's combined knowledge of latex foam technology, they established Vitafoam in 1949 with only £100 capital, manufacturing cushion units and mattresses on the ground floor of Glen Mill in Oldham with first year sales totalling £102,000. Vitafoam's success was also attributable to other early colleagues including Alf Broadbent and Fred Whitehead who both made a major contribution to the development of the company, with Fernley Parker giving financial and accounting advice.

However several hurdles were to follow. The Korean War in the 1950s caused rubber prices to soar. Then prices slumped, profits were wiped out

Above: Norman Grimshaw (left) founder of Vitafoam Limited, which developed into today's multi-national British Vita PLC. He is pictured here, during his army days with Fernley Parker.
Left: The Glen Mill, scene of Vitafoam's first business operation.

and the business had to begin all over again. None-the-less, with enthusiasm from both management and employees, together with strong leadership, the team quickly had the business back on its feet. Production soon expanded and within four years, it occupied a further two floors and a cellar at Glen Mill and it was at this time that Fernley Parker came on board fully to head up the accounting and finance function. Shortly after, the Don Mill in Middleton was purchased and became the new headquarters and production unit.

Within a further four years, more mills, Soudan 1 and 2 were acquired and Vitafoam now had a highly concentrated factory layout of more than half a million square feet. Next came international involvement. With extensive travelling by Messrs Grimshaw and Parker, partnerships were set up on a 50/50 basis in developing areas whereby established companies in overseas countries supplied local marketing knowledge and sales organisation whilst Vita provided plant, technical and financial advice and training. The first associate company in Southern Rhodesia (now Zimbabwe) was formed in 1960 and deals were done with several African countries until the 1970s when currency problems meant that very little cash could be returned to the UK.

Diversifying from latex foam to polyurethanes and solid polymers in the 1960s, Vita extended its markets from furnishing into carpet underlays, the automotive industry and a variety of other outlets before going

public as British Vita Company Ltd. in 1967. Continental Europe was the next area for expansion following the purchase of Caligen Foam in Accrington which brought with it a sister company in Holland. Today, the company possesses more than 150 operations across Western and Eastern Europe, North America, Canada, Australasia and Africa with a developing interest in the Far East. Its manufacturing capabilities, too, have grown extensively from natural and synthetic foams to include solid and liquid compounding, thermoplastic extrusion and a wide range of synthetic fibre and fabric materials. Its influence is present in products from all the major industries including engineering, transportation, furnishing, bedding, medical, apparel, packaging, leisure and building.

Certainly, British Vita has grown far larger than Mr. Grimshaw or any of his early colleagues had ever envisaged. With a turnover now in excess of £1bn and a workforce of 13,000, the company is uniquely placed to take advantage of the seemingly limitless applications for the materials it processes and perfectly positioned to welcome the challenges and meet customers' needs as it enters the 21st century.

Above: Continuous moulding tracks for latex foam cushioning, at one time without equal in the UK, were produced at Vita's Middleton site.
Left: Gracie Fields, complete with handbag, conducts the band during the official opening of Vitool in October 1970.

Almost a hundred years of growth through technology

Chadwick Web Processing, at Century Works, Webster Street was founded in 1907 by a local engineer, Cobden Chadwick. Cobden gained his engineering skills whilst working for his father, Joseph in the family business. He repaired and maintained the firm's bag making machines.

He started his own bag making machine repair firm in a tiny one storey building just off West Street in Oldham, using only the basic machinery, such as old belt driven machine tools with very simple motors for a power source. It was natural that Cobden would follow the line of business he was familiar with. This was fine for a while but Cobden had ambition. It was natural progression from repairing and maintaining the bag making machines to manufacturing them.

He hit upon the idea that many companies were crying out for paper bags to advertise their products and he developed a bag machine that

had a single colour letterpress machine attached which enabled companies to commission him to print their advertising on the bags. This proved an enormous success. So much so, in fact, that he was able to move to larger premises at Gravel Walks, near Mumps Bridge twelve months later. In the mid 1920s a two colour bag machine and printer was introduced.

Cobden's son, John had shown a great interest in the firm since his childhood and when Cobden decided to take things a little easier in 1937, his son took over as managing director, remaining in this position until 1968.

Just prior to the war the firm moved again to its present address at Century Works, Webster Street.

The direction of the company changed dramatically during the Second World War, perhaps as a decline in demand from customers who had less money to spend on advertising. During this difficult time the firm specialised in manufacturing machine tools but after the conflict it returned to its initial function, adding to this the introduction of manufacture of printing presses and reel-to-reel presses.

A four colour printing machine with a rewind function for Christmas and other wrapping papers was one early invention.

Above: Gravel Street, to which the company moved in 1908.
Left: A 1970s picture of the machinery used.

The common single impression cylinder press was designed in the 1960s. This was a great development for the company and the printing industry as a whole as it meant better colour-to-colour registration.

In 1968 John became Chairman and his son, Peter took over as managing director. During this time the single impression cylinder press was further developed, becoming more sophisticated as new enhancements were adopted.

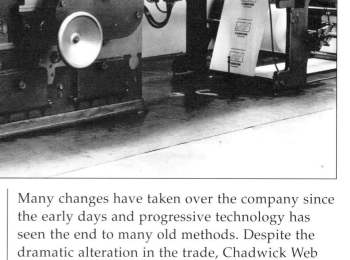

Although it is not unknown for three generations of a family to work together for a company, what is unusual is the level of involvement shown with this firm. On one occasion, the father of a family was sent (by his son who was the production manager at the time) to clean out a water tank. The man subsequently fell in and his screams for help were heard by his grandson, who fished him out. What was overheard then is unprintable.

Many changes have taken over the company since the early days and progressive technology has seen the end to many old methods. Despite the dramatic alteration in the trade, Chadwick Web Processing remains a private company.

One of the main reasons that the company has survived over the years is the high quality and excellence in engineering as well as attentiveness to customer needs. ISO 9001 was awarded as a result of this. A major part of the sales are exported worldwide with a sales and service office in Green Bay, Wisconsin, USA as well as 30 agents based all over the world.

This achievement gained the firm the Queen's Award for Export. Without this continual development and urge to excel in every way, the company could never have come this far. And because of this, Chadwicks is ensured a place in the new millennium as a 'local firm made good'.

Above: An exhibition from the early 1960s.
Left: This picture is probably best dated by the fashions worn. This machine dates from the 1970s.

A good yarn for the world

Knoll Spinning is based at New Wellington Mills in Greenfield, near Oldham. The original mill was built in 1852 for Shaw, Son & Lees, local cotton spinners who traded until 1858. They were succeeded in the mill by N. Broadbent & Sons who carried on the cotton spinning tradition until their departure in 1932. The mill was left vacant for six years, after which time part of it was used for general engineering works. In 1941 part of the premises were opened up with the installation of 362 looms by the cotton fabric weaver, B. Kershaw.

Peter Fox - 'Old Saddleworth' Collection

The birth of the Knoll Spinning Company

During the war years the engineering section of the mill produced engine parts for Mosquito Bomber aircraft, after which time it became firstly a naval stores and then a storage base for the British Wool Board. In 1946, William Oddy, a Shipley weaver bought the buildings and land (with the exception of one small building off Wellington Road). They transferred all their woollen carding and mule spinning operations from Shipley to the mill.

The Knoll Spinning Company was born. It was so named to allow commission spinning to take place without actually involving Oddy's name. The name 'Knoll', meaning 'small hill' came from Oddy's house name.

The first carding machines were installed in 1946 and by 1951 all fourteen operating machines were either replaced completely or re-equipped to form virtually new machines. This investment in modern technology has been on-going ever since. At this time, yarns were produced for woven wear and hosiery. Later, in 1952, worsted drawing and spinning machines were installed to make yarns for William Oddy, who had kept up a separate enterprise in Shipley, manufacturing fabrics with worsted warps and woollen wefts. It was during that year that Knoll was registered as a separate subsidiary of William Oddy's.

Take-over

Disaster struck in 1955 when Number One Mill, originally five storeys high, was burnt to the ground. It was rebuilt quickly, minus two storeys and all the worsted machines destroyed in the blaze were replaced. In addition, by 1956 a new pneumatic blending plant was built with hydraulic mules and twisting frames being installed as well. This meant that the company was one of

Oldham Chronicle

Above and left: Two images of Wellington Mill, the one above dating from when it was built and the one on the left from just prior to the fire which destroyed most of the mill in the foreground.

the most technologically advanced of its kind in the world.
In 1960 William Oddy along with Knoll Spinning were both acquired by the Parkland Group. This led to further capital investment during the early 1960s, seeing the whole worsted spinning unit being re-equipped with the most up-to-date machinery. This policy of replacement continued throughout the decade until in 1970, all worsted spinning operations at Knoll were stopped and the machinery moved to other plants within the Parkland Group. From then on, Knoll concentrated on the knitwear market.

It proved to be a wise move. In 1975 Knoll was recognised for its achievements in export, by winning the acclaimed Queen's Award to Industry. The continuing advancements in technology and management were further recognised in 1987 by the company's success in being the first woollen spinner to win acceptance as a British Standards Institute registered company.

And today...

In 1997 Knoll unveiled a £750,000 blending plant which included new state-of-the-art machinery which promises to make the company Europe's leader in blending technology. This was a major investment for Knoll and the technical capabilities offered by the plant combined with traditional expertise, will ensure that Knoll enters the 21st century equipped to meet the changing demands of the knitwear industry in the UK and abroad.

Above: The fire in 1955 in Number One Mill destroyed the building. It was later rebuilt three storeys high.
Left: This picture dates from 1963 and shows the managing director of Knoll at the time, Mr H Bentley discussing a new blend with Mr E Royston.

Her Majesty Queen Elizabeth II 's visit to Oldham in October 1954.

ACKNOWLEDGMENTS

THE PUBLISHERS WOULD LIKE TO THANK THE
FOLLOWING PEOPLE AND ORGANISATIONS FOR THEIR
HELP IN THE PRODUCTION OF THIS BOOK.

LOUISE KARLSEN AND TERRY BERRY
OF OLDHAM LOCAL STUDIES LIBRARY

PHILIP HIRST, EDITOR
OLDHAM EVENING CHRONICLE